OUR WORTHY COMMANDER

the life and times

of

BENJAMIN K. PIERCE

in whose honor

FORT PIERCE

was named

BENJAMIN KENDRICK PIERCE

1790 — 1850

Photograph of the original painting from Mrs. Meeta Meyers Bouchette, Ottawa, Canada, great, great granddaughter of Benjamin K. Pierce and Josephine La Framboise.

OUR WORTHY COMMANDER

the life and times

of

BENJAMIN K. PIERCE

in whose honor

FORT PIERCE

was named

by

LOUIS H. BURBEY

The Indian River Community College
Historical Data Center

IRCC PIONEER PRESS
FORT PIERCE, FLORIDA
1976

Published by the
Indian River Community College Historical Data Center

FORT PIERCE, FLORIDA 33450
IRCC PIONEER PRESS

Printed in the United States of America

LIBRARY OF CONGRESS CATALOG CARD NUMBER 76-5992

DEDICATED TO

*The friendly, hospitable people
of Fort Pierce, Florida*

Acknowledgement

Appreciation is expressed to those who have generously assisted in the publishing of the biography of Benjamin K. Pierce by providing access to manuscripts, published works, and other reference material, or by aiding in the research and preparation of the manuscript.

Especially, I would like to thank Mr. James M. Halbe, whose cooperation in locating and obtaining valuable letters and other information contributed much to the completeness of this Pierce biography.

Special recognition and appreciation are due also to the New Hampshire Historical Society, the Wisconsin Historical Society, the Michigan Historical Society, the Tampa Historical Society, the Florida Historical Society, the St. Lucie County Historical Society, the Pensacola Historical Society, the St. Augustine Historical Society, the Oakland County Historical Society, the Birmingham Historical Society, and the Mackinac Island Historical Society; and to the Burton Historical Collections of the main library in Detroit and to the National Archives in Washington, D.C.

Gratitude is also extended to Mr. Harry W. Blake, Superintendent of the Cypress Hills National Cemetery, and to Mrs. A. H. Bouchette, Ottawa, Canada, the great, great granddaughter of Benjamin K. Pierce and his wife Josephine.

Thanks are due to the Indian River Community College Historical Data Center for undertaking the publication of this biography; and to Mr. Gene Lyon, Mrs. Ada Coats Williams, Mr. Joseph Colville, Mr. Reginald Woodall, and Dr. Rudolph P. Widman, who all worked with me to complete the final work.

Louis H. Burbey

Royal Oak, Michigan

Foreward

The publication of this biography has been undertaken by the Indian River Community College Historical Data Center in accepting its responsibility to the community and advancing the knowledge of history.

The Indian River Community College Historical Data Center was started to aid all local historical associations in their efforts to collect historical materials relating to St. Lucie, Martin, Indian River, and Okeechobee counties. It was through this mission that Louis H. Burbey, a retired Detroit newspaperman and historian, donated his research, documents, and Benjamin K. Pierce Manuscript to the college.

While writing a local history series for a Birmingham, Michigan, newspaper, Mr. Burbey became interested in the origin of Birmingham street names, among them Pierce Street. Research of early land purchase records showed that Benjamin K. Pierce was a pioneer land purchaser; hence, Pierce Street and nearby Pierce High School were named in his honor.

A frequent winter visitor to Florida since 1933, Burbey, following further research on Pierce's military career, became interested in a possible connection between Pierce in Michigan and Fort Pierce, Florida. Further inquiries led him to James Halbe, of Fort Pierce, who had also done extensive research on Benjamin K. Pierce. An exchange of information, references, and documents resulted in an exceptionally detailed accumulation of facts which were extended into this complete and authentic biography.

Several people were instrumental in making this biography a reality. Joe Colville and Ada Coats Williams spent considerable time working with Louis Burbey to coordinate the original manuscript and to edit the final product. Dr. Herman A. Heise, President of Indian

River Community College, had the foresight to originate the Historical Data Center at the college and to encourage the final publication of this biography.

We trust that you will enjoy this account of the life and times of Benjamin K. Pierce and appreciate its historical contribution.

Rudolph P. Widman, Ph.D.

Fort Pierce, Florida
April, 1976

TABLE OF CONTENTS

I   The Cause and The Effect 1

II   The Second Seminole War 5

III   Benjamin K. Pierce — Family Background 9

IV   The War of 1812 13

V   After the Treaty of Ghent 19

VI   Mackinac Island — 1816-1818 25

VII   Mackinac Island — 1818-1820 29

VIII   Fort San Carlos De Barrancas - Pensacola, Florida 35

IX   Fort Delaware 37

X   Second Florida Assignment: Fort Defiance 41

XI   The Battle of Wahoo Swamp 47

XII   Northern Assignment 51

XIII   Third Florida Assignment: Indian River Inlet 55

XIV   Return to Michigan 61

XV   The Final Years 65

XVI   People in Pierce's Life 69

XVII   Benjamin K. Pierce — A Summary 75

References 79

Bibliography 81

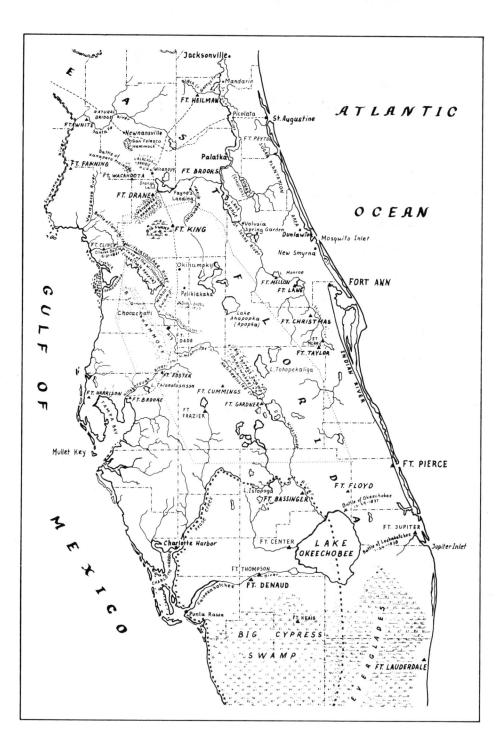

I THE CAUSE AND
THE EFFECT

The many people who annually come to glamorous Florida to bask in its glorious sunshine and enjoy its many fabulous recreational facilities have little time to think of Florida's earlier days when it was a primitive wilderness, which, actually, was not so long ago.

Visitors and newly settled residents hear of the more or less legendary Asi-Ya-Hola (Osceola) and the Seminole Indians who in some way seem to be associated with Florida's past. For a better understanding of the events narrated in the following chapters, it is best to briefly outline the dramatic and tragic part that destiny ordained the Seminoles to play in Florida's bygone days, their influence on the life of Benjamin K. Pierce, and, in the final analysis, the beginning of what is today the city of Fort Pierce.

Generally speaking, the Seminole Indians referred to in this narrative were an amalgamation of diverse groups, mostly Creek Indian sub-tribes, such as the Mikasuki and Muskogee, originally from the Georgia country and beyond. The earlier history of the various tribes which eventually merged into the Seminole family was a turbulent one. They were involved not only in inter-tribal warfare, but were involved, sometimes as allies, sometimes as foes, with the three nations who at one time or another controlled or sought to control the country: Spain, Great Britain, and the United States.

For numerous reasons, among them British intrigue during the War of 1812, the sub-tribes were in almost constant conflict with the Americans along the central Florida border from about 1811. In the second decade of the 1800's, the United States troops and various militia units engaged in a series of conflicts with the central Florida natives in what has been termed the First Seminole War. On the pretext of safeguarding the borders of the United States, American troops had no compunction about invading Spain's Florida lands to destroy native forts and settlements.

The result of that conflict was Spain's decision to salvage whatever possible out of its untenable, poorly protected, and profitless property. By treaty, February 22, 1819, ratified in 1821, Spain ceded Florida to the United States in exchange for government assumption of $5,000,000 in claims by American citizens against Spain. In 1822 the Seminoles, now more or less concentrated on the upper portion of Florida's peninsula, came under the jurisdiction of the American government when Florida became a Territory of the United States.

Under American rule the Seminole situation was a pathetic one. Defeated, they had become impoverished wanderers, reduced in numbers, and with no status as a nation, tribe, or people. They were not consulted, and their rights were entirely overlooked in the negotiations by which the United States acquired Florida from Spain. Although weak and poor, "their native spirit [was] not so much broken as to humble them to the dust."

As adventurers, traders, land speculators, and settlers trekked into the new American possession, prior tensions and resentments mounted between the invaders and the natives. What to do with the Seminoles became a torrid issue. The great concern was how to get them out of the way of the advancing white man.

Many solutions were devised and attempted but proved unsatisfactory, unworkable, and unacceptable to the natives. Finally, the decision to move them to new lands west of the Mississippi was made by Congress on April 8, 1834. The moving of the Seminole Nation from Florida was to be completed by April 12, 1836.

The majority of the Seminoles vehemently protested the decision. When they were threatened to be expelled by force if necessary, they quietly prepared to resist by stocking up on powder and ball. The determination of the Seminoles to remain in Florida is well illustrated by the death of Charley Emathla, a chief of a sub-tribe who was making preparations to accept the white man's proposal and move west. He was shot and killed by the fiery Osceola.

Osceola, a thirty-one-year-old Creek-Muskogee Seminole, supposedly with a strain of Scotch and Spanish blood, a natural-born leader but not a chief, was a major factor in cementing the Indian resistance movement. In military reports Osceola was referred to as "Powell" or "the renegade, half-breed Powell," which was incorrect. Osceola acquired the "Powell" after his father died, through the marriage of his mother to a trader, William Powell.

If early historians are correct, Osceola's extreme hatred of the white man can be partially attributed to the unjust seizure of his wife by hypothetical representatives of northern slave-owners. His wife, a Seminole with some Negro blood, was presumably the granddaughter of an escaped slave, and consequently was considered legitimate prey for seizure under Federal rulings.

In June, 1835, while attending a conference at Fort King (near Ocala) and as a result of a heated argument over the Seminole problems, Indian Agent Wiley Thompson arrested Osceola and confined him in irons for six days under guard at the fort. That insult to the proud leader was an important influence in the eruption of the Second Seminole War, a conflict in which Osceola played a vital role and attained a national reputation. Today, the "smiling, affable and courtly" Osceola, intensely patriotic to the Seminole cause, has acquired the status of a legendary hero in Florida history.

Chapter: 25

On the morning of the ... January 1838 we
moved over to the west side of Indian river;
...
...
...
...
...
...
...
it was therefore dubbed Fort Pierce
after our ... commander ...

II   THE SECOND
SEMINOLE WAR

Florida's Second Seminole War burst into the open with a dramatic and tragic suddenness in December, 1835. On December 18, eight Seminoles under the leadership of Osceola ambushed and captured a United States military wagon baggage detachment north of the present city of Micanopy, so named after a prominent Indian chief.

On December 28, eight United States Army officers and 100 regulars under the command of Major Francis L. Dade, marching along a faint trail from Fort Brooks (Tampa) to Fort King (Ocala), were ambushed and annihilated.* On the afternoon of the same day, Osceola, previously arrested and chained by Indian Agent Wiley Thompson, retrieved his honor and satisfied his vengeance by ambushing and killing Thompson and his companion, Lieutenant Constantine Smith, as they strolled outside the palisades of Fort King. Nearby, Osceola's companions surprised and shot the fort's sutler, Erastus Rogers, and his two clerks.

Inspired by the leadership of the dauntless Osceola, the Seminoles raided and destroyed plantations, villages, and lone settlers' homes; and the inhabitants, in most cases, were killed. Frustrated government officials and generals found the wiley Seminoles a difficult enemy to combat. Following their hit-and-run guerilla tactics, the Seminoles disappeared into Florida's many lake and swamp regions, retiring to isolated, well-established and difficult-to-approach hammock villages to recuperate and prepare for their next attack.

In two years of warfare, many skirmishes and battles took place with heavy losses on both sides. Commands were shifted, and troops were replaced and augmented with no significant decisive results. In 1837, the number of United States forces on Florida's peninsula had escalated to approximately 9,000 men. Four thousand six hundred and thirty-six regulars, more than half the regular United States Army, were in remote Florida, engaged in this new kind of undeclared guerilla war.

*The present Dade County and Dade City were named in honor of Major Francis L. Dade.

Vehement northern public opinion in opposition to the war, accentuated by the apparent lack of success and stalemated situation, finally resulted in a plan which called for a complete sweep of Florida's peninsula from coast to coast by several army units.

In December, 1837, coordinated with the drive to the South, a navy artillery detachment was bivouacked on a prairie at the northern end of the Indian River, where Fort Ann had been erected. The fort was named by Lieutenant Erwin, the architect and builder, "after the prettiest girl in Pennsylvania."

On December 26, Lieutenant L. M. Powell, in command of the navy unit, sailed down the Indian River on an exploring expedition, seeking favorable sites for supply depots. On December 30, the artillery unit followed:

> *. . . quietly gliding down Indian River . . . as we had a fair wind . . . . we did not check our career but continued all night under easy sail. . . . at 4 o'clock in the afternoon of the 31st Dec'r, we reached Indian River Inlet, 90 miles south of Ft. Ann. We there found Lt. Powell and his command encamped near the sea-beach.[1]*

Attached to the Artillery command was an army surgeon, Jacob R. Motte, who, in his Journal, recorded the activities of his unit following the reunion:

> *We pitched our tents upon the white sands of the sea-shore. On the morning of the 2nd January, 1838, we moved over to the west side of the Indian River, to a spot four miles south of the inlet, designated as the 'bluff,' par excellence, being the highest point of land on the whole river, though only about ten or fifteen feet above the water. We there established ourselves; first by pitching our tents on a narrow esplanade between the river and the bluff, which rises perpendicularly behind us; next by erecting a block-house upon the top of bluff. Being pretty much like all other block-houses in Florida except that this one was built of palmetto logs, we deemed it worthy the title of a fort, and the distinction of a name; it was therefore dubbed Fort Pierce, after our worthy commander.[2]*

From this routine and peaceful military episode of the violent Second Seminole War, Fort Pierce came into existence as a military supply depot and as a place-name, destined eventually to become the location and name of the city of Fort Pierce.

Apparently, New Year's Day, January 1, 1838, was a day of rest and relaxation. According to Motte:

> *At reveille next morning, New Year's Day, I was up, and with several of my brother officers proceeded immediately to the beach for a bath . . . with the thermometer at 80⁰, we did not apprehend much danger from taking cold. . . . After breakfast, the morning was devoted to a stroll along the beach.*

A conjecture of the observance of the New Year by the troops would be that, following an extra ration of liquor by their "worthy commander," they regaled themselves on the "quantity and quality of the fish that abounded in those waters . . . of the finest flavor and of large dimensions . . . . As for the oysters, six are a comfortable meal for one person; indeed without exaggeration, the greatest abundance may be easily obtained." Motte recorded that, in the days following, "[we] began to grow so fat that we were afraid unless something turned up very soon to produce a change in our felicitous mode of life, that we should have had to borrow from our neighbors, the Indians, their style of dress, for our clothes every day became tighter."

In commemoration of this event at Indian River Inlet, January 1, 1838, an "Auld Lang Syne" each New Year's Day to the spirits of those brave men who came to Fort Pierce in the long ago: a vote of thanks to Army Surgeon Jacob R. Motte, who recorded the details; and a brief memoriam for Daniel Haggerty, Private, Company A, who, United States Army records state: "died, Fort Pierce, Jan. 3, 1838; disease unknown"; likewise, Daniel Collins, Private, Company F, who "died, Ft. Pierce, Feb. 12, 1838; disease unknown." Somewhere, perhaps, their bones lie undisturbed near the site of the palmetto blockhouse which was dubbed Fort Pierce after Our Worthy Commander.

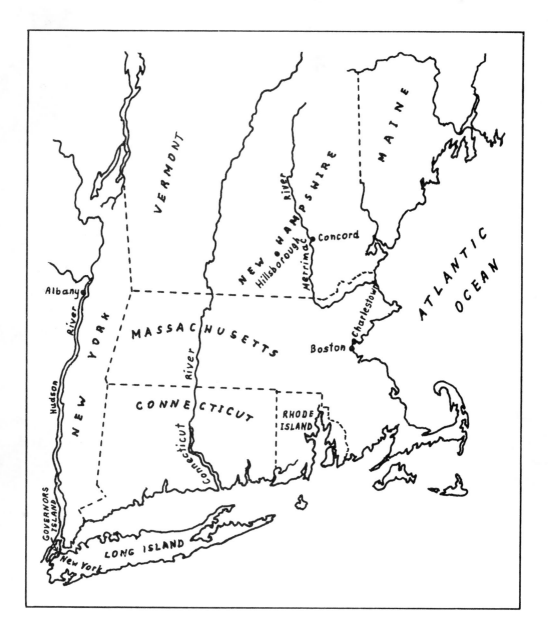

III BENJAMIN K. PIERCE - FAMILY BACKGROUND

Until recently, only brief facts were known about the worthy commander of the troops who erected the palmetto log blockhouse, which they named in his honor. For some strange reason he was relegated to comparative oblivion, historically speaking. Perhaps one reason for the neglect can be attributed to the fact that interest in the Pierce family as a whole was focused on Franklin Pierce, the worthy commander's younger brother, who, in 1853, was inaugurated as the fourteenth President of the United States.

Whatever reason for the years of oversight, Fort Pierce's namesake has every right to shine in the glory of his own accomplishments. Musty army records, old newspapers, letters, and varied fragments of information gathered from scores of scattered locations reveal a dedicated professional soldier and patriot, who during turbulent times in the early history of the United States made greater sacrifices and contributed more to his country in many ways than his more famous brother.

The worthy commander of the troops at Indian River Inlet on New Year's Day, 1838, was Lieutenant Colonel Benjamin Kendrick Pierce, descendant of a distinguished line of Pierces dating back to the original immigrants, Thomas Pierce and his wife Elizabeth, both born in England. They, with several children, settled at Charlestown, Massachusetts, about 1633–34, where they and their immediate descendants acquired considerable stature in their area.

Benjamin K. Pierce actually was Benjamin III in the family. His grandfather was named Benjamin, likewise his father, who was born at Chelmsford, Massachusetts, December 25, 1757, where he resided in his early life and was known as an industrious and thrifty farmer.

According to the Massachusetts Revoluntionary Rolls, Benjamin II, immediately after the Battle of Lexington, April 19, 1775, enlisted at the age of eighteen in Colonel Brooks' Regiment, participated in the Battle of Bunker Hill, and was cited for bravery in several

9

other engagements, particularly the Battle of Bemis Heights.

After eight years of service in the American War for Independence, he retired with the rank of Brevet-Major. It is recorded that while a prisoner of the British at New York he was "grossly insulted by a British officer whom he ran through the body in a duel." Following the disbanding of the Patriot Army, he bought a tract of forest land in Hillsborough County, New Hampshire, on which he settled in 1786 and cleared for a farm.

On May 24, 1787, he married Elizabeth Andrews, who died the following year, August 3, 1788, leaving a daughter Elizabeth, who eventually became the wife of General John McNeil, a War of 1812 veteran. Both of them had an important role in the life of Benjamin K. Pierce.

On February 1, 1790, the senior Pierce married Anna Kendrick "of the illustrious Kendricks." The first born of this second marriage is the subject of this biography; Benjamin Kendrick Pierce, born August 29, 1790. The "Kendrick" obviously was derived from his mother's maiden name.

Three more sons and three daughters were born of this marriage. John Sullivan, born November 5, 1796, became a United States Army officer, was stationed at Mackinac Island, Michigan, following the War of 1812, and died at Detroit, Michigan, September 4, 1824, leaving his wife and two children.

The other sons were Henry D. and Franklin (who was born November 23, 1804). Franklin entered politics; and was a member of Congress (1833–37), a United States Senator (1837–42), and Brigadier General in the United States-Mexican War (1846–48); was nominated for President at the Democratic Convention in 1852; and was elected the fourteenth President of the United States.

The elder Pierce was a member of the New Hampshire State Legislature for thirteen years and was elected Governor of New Hampshire in 1827 and re-elected in 1829. In the fall of 1786, he was commissioned a Major in the militia of Hillsborough County, promoted to Colonel "for the great value of his services," and in 1805 was appointed Brigadier General of militia. As a result of his public and military services he was usually referred to as "General" or "Governor."

In 1836 Benjamin K. Pierce's father was elected vice-president of the Massachusetts "Society (Order) of the Cincinnati," the oldest military society in America, founded May 13, 1783, by officers of the Continental Army. George Washington was the society's first president. Benjamin K. Pierce also became a member of this society, the exact date unknown. Many of Benjamin K.'s fellow officers were members, as well as many notables, such as United States Presidents, including his brother Franklin.

General Pierce (or Governor Pierce, however one prefers to refer to him) died at Hillsborough, April 1, 1839, at age eighty-two. His obituary notices state: "He was a man of great native talent . . . a leader of men. . . . Without the advantages of early education, without opulent and powerful friends . . . he grew to be the most influential man in New Hampshire."

There was a closely knit family association between Benjamin K. Pierce, his father and mother, his brother Franklin, and particularly his half-sister, Elizabeth, and her husband, General John McNeil. In the many letters exchanged between them, Benjamin K. time after time expressed his deep gratitude to Elizabeth and the General for the many favors and assistance rendered.

One of the tragic phases of Benjamin K.'s life was his loss of three wives, all by natural causes. The support, care, and education of his children, as a consequence of those bereavements, were a constant worry to him. Military pay in Pierce's time can not be regarded as generous.

This resumé of Benjamin K. Pierce's family background is an essential part of his biography; for the many family letters and records of his prominent father, his famous brother, and notable relatives furnish the more intimate sources of information of the details of Benjamin K.'s life as a husband, father, and officer. The city of Fort Pierce, Florida, can take great pride in its association with the illustrious Pierce family of long ago.

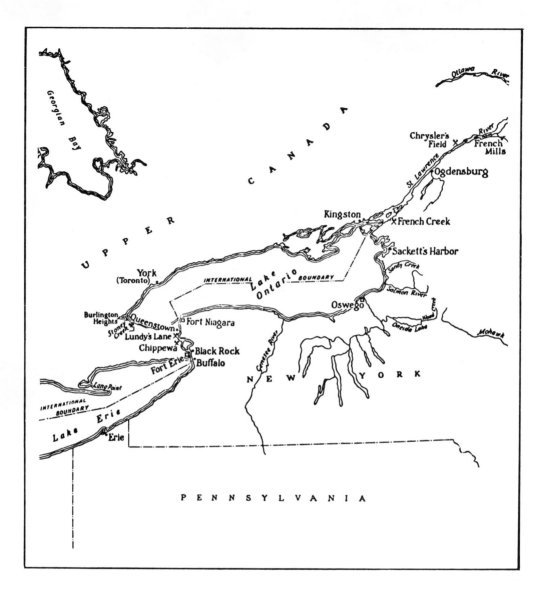

IV   THE WAR OF 1812

No information so far has been found regarding the boyhood of Benjamin K. Pierce. His father, denied the advantage of early schooling and self-educated, "was much more sensitive to the want of education than others." Consequently, he apparently made available whatever opportunities there were for a proper and early education of his family.

It is recorded, however, that Benjamin K. Pierce

pursued his preparatory studies at Philips Exeter Academy, entered Dartmouth College, in the fall of 1807, at age seventeen, and continued in that institution for three years. He then commenced the study of law with David Starret, Esq., of Hillsborough and continued in Mr. Starret's office until the commencement of the War of 1812 with Great Britain, when he entered the regular army as a lieutenant of artillery.

Consequently, Pierce received three years of advanced education and two years of law study. Obviously his intent was to follow the practice of law. However, similar to others of his age and time, he gave up his studies; and on March 12, 1812, at the age of 22, he enlisted in the United States Army four months before the official commencement of the war. His service record shows that he was commissioned a First Lieutenant, and that he was assigned to the Third Regiment of Artillery. This active artillery association he was to hold for thirty-eight years, except for several tours of short, detached, special military duties.

Incidental to Pierce's enlistment is this bit of information from his father's obituary notice in the *Farmer's Monthly Visitor:* "His sons, Benjamin Kendrick and John Sullivan the youngest of which was in his minority, by advice of their father at once entered the military service."[3] This was not an unexpected sort of advice in view of the Pierce family's previous distinguished military service.

Important to much of Benjamin K. Pierce's future military activities and personal interests is the fact that he began his military career under the command of Alexander Macomb, who was born at Detroit, Michigan, April 3, 1782, while Michigan was under

13

British rule. Macomb, of a wealthy, prominent, and pioneer Detroit family, was one of West Point's first graduates; and at the Battle of Plattsburg, September 6–11, 1814, he became a national hero by defeating, in conjunction with Commodore McDonnough, "the strongest force Great Britain ever sent against the United States." At the outset of the Second Seminole War, General Macomb was commander-in-chief of the United States Army, a position he held until his death in 1841.

Macomb obviously observed some superior quality and ability in young Lieutenant Pierce, as indicated by a letter from Pierce to his father, postmarked Albany, New York, and dated December 12, 1812:

> *A short time since I wrote you from Sackett's Harbor on Lake Ontario. Soon after the date of that, I unexpectedly received orders from Col. Macomb to attend him on a visit to this city where I now am. . . . The troops have generally repaired to winter quarters. There will therefore be nothing done towards the conquest of Canada, only to keep up the recruiting service, increasing the regular force and preparing for a spring campaign. . . . I shall proceed tomorrow on my way to the city of New York with Col. Macomb.*

Included in the letter was a request by Pierce on the care of his horse which he was sending to the charge of his father:

> *I wish to have particular care taken of him as he is a most beautiful animal. I would by no means have him rode by any person except yourself. . . . When he arrives at Hillsborough it will be 800 miles that he has been rode with scarcely resting.*

Little things in life such as this often best disclose the character of an individual.

From that letter it appears Macomb had assigned Lieutenant Pierce to recruiting duty in New York, an assignment which was to continue through the winter of 1812–13, in preparation, as Pierce stated, for a spring campaign. In later years and at various posts of duty, Pierce engaged in many recruiting activities, a function in which he appears to have been particularly qualified. Likewise, he was assigned court-martial duties, a result, no doubt, of his early law training.

The activities of Pierce in the War of 1812 are difficult to trace in the National Archives because of the lack of compiled Pierce service records or document file; therefore, in reply to requests: "We cannot state positively the battles in which he participated."

It appears that Lieutenant Pierce served in the First Battalion of his regiment (Third Artillery), which was assigned during the War of 1812 to the Northern Military Division, which participated in many engagements with the British along the eastern length of the Canadian – United States border west to Michigan.

Two companies of the Third Regiment participated in the Battle of Queenstown

Heights, October 12, 1812, while detachments of the Third Regiment saw action at Fort Niagara, November 21, 1812. Whether Lieutenant Pierce was involved in those activities remains unanswered. However, it was following those engagements that he was selected by Macomb to accompany him to New York, where he was assigned to recruiting duty.

On October 1, 1813, Lieutenant Pierce was promoted to Captain and assigned to the command of an artillery company on December 12, 1813. In March, 1814, Captain Pierce and his unit apparently were under the command of General Jacob Brown.

The objective of the British in the spring of 1814 was to gain control of Lake Ontario, which led to the attack on Oswego, at the mouth of the Oswego River, on May 5 and 6. One of the few actual service records of Pierce so far located in the National Archives carried this brief notation: "Commanding company in engagement with enemy at Oswego."

According to historian Lossing, the first attempt of the British to capture Fort Ontario, situated on a high bluff above the village of Oswego, was repulsed by a heavy cannon placed near the shore. They attacked again "and were compelled to ascend a long, steep hill in the face of heavy fire" by the Americans. The American troops, however, were finally obliged to abandon Fort Ontario. They retreated to a woods, where Colonel Mitchell attacked the front of the advancing British, "while the remainder of his command under Captains McIntrye and Pierce annoyed them prodigiously on the flank."

The finale to the engagement: "By desperate fighting the enemy was kept in check for a long time, but overwhelming numbers compelled Mitchell to fall back" ten miles up the Oswego River to Oswego Falls, the site of a naval supply depot.

After the Battle of Oswego, records show Captain Pierce at Sackett's Harbor at various times during 1814. His periodic absences may be accounted for by the following engagements in which Captain Pierce's Corps of Artillery participated in that year: July 3, Fort Erie; July 5, Chippewa, Upper Canada; July 25, Lundy's Lane (Niagara Falls). At Lundy's Lane, Pierce's brother-in-law, Colonel John McNeil (Infantry) was wounded in both legs by cannister shot, shattering his right knee and crippling him for life.

In the September 6–11 Battle of Plattsburg, in which various artillery units saw action, Alexander Macomb attained his fame. He was awarded a gold medal from Congress and was promoted to Major General. It is logical to assume that Captain Pierce's artillery unit saw action in at least one or more of those 1814 battles, but no record has been located so far to verify any assumption.

The Treaty of Ghent (signed December 24, 1814, ratified, and proclaimed February 18, 1815) officially terminated the War of 1812 between England and the United States. This completed the first chapter in the military career of Captain Benjamin K. Pierce. Many of Pierce's fellow officers in that war—Gaines, Clinch, and Jesup, for example—appeared two decades later in Florida's Second Seminole War.

The Battle of Oswego
In 1814, Captain B. K. Pierce engaged British troops in New York at the Oswego River.

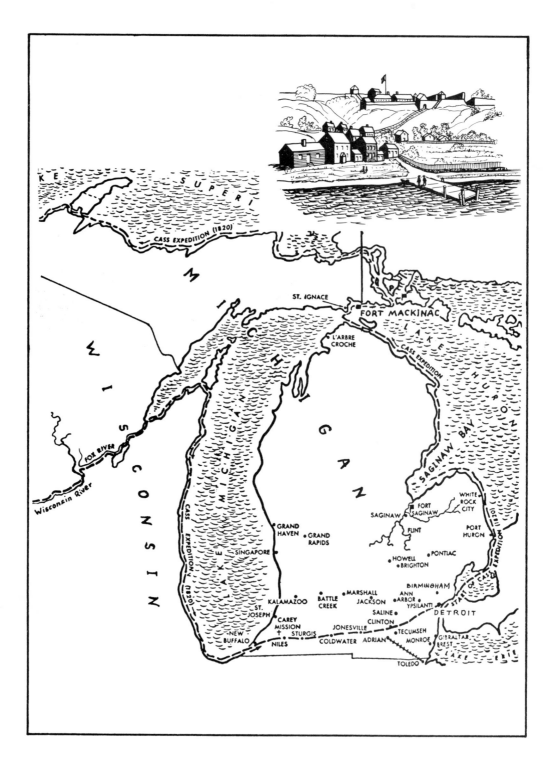

LAKE SUPERIOR

KE

SUPERI

CASS EXPEDITION (1820)

M I C H I G A N

WISCONSIN

FOX RIVER

Wisconsin River

LAKE MICHIGAN

ST. IGNACE

FORT MACKINAC

L'ARBRE CROCHE

LAKE HURON

CASS EXPEDITION

SAGINAW BAY

Saginaw

FORT SAGINAW

WHITE ROCK CITY

FLINT

PORT HURON

GRAND HAVEN

GRAND RAPIDS

HOWELL

BRIGHTON

PONTIAC

SINGAPORE

BIRMINGHAM

CASS EXPEDITION (1820)

BATTLE CREEK

MARSHALL

JACKSON

ANN ARBOR

YPSILANTI

START OF CASS EXPEDITION

KALAMAZOO

ST. JOSEPH

SALINE

CLINTON

DETROIT

CAREY MISSION

STURGIS

JONESVILLE

TECUMSEH

NEW BUFFALO

NILES

COLDWATER

ADRIAN

MONROE

GIBRALTAR BREST

LAKE

TOLEDO

V AFTER THE TREATY
OF GHENT

In the May 17, 1815, peacetime reorganization of the United States Army, various regiments of dragoons and infantry were consolidated with Captain Pierce's basic unit, the Corps of Artillery. It was complicated, however, by each branch of the service maintaining its original identity. Under those arrangements it appears that Pierce was in command of Company O, First Battalion, Fourth Regiment, with Company O retaining its status as an artillery unit. Under the reorganization, General Macomb was assigned to the command of Military District Five, with headquarters at Detroit, Michigan.

Detroit had been captured by the British during the War of 1812, but at the time of Macomb's return it was safely back in American possession. However, Mackinac Island and Fort Mackinac (300 miles north of Detroit at the head of Lake Huron), likewise captured in the war, were still occupied by British troops awaiting United States repossession according to the Treaty of Ghent.

From Wood's *Historic Mackinac:*

British troops, Col. McDouall in command, occupied Fort Mackinac until noon July 18, 1815, when they were relieved by United States troops consisting of two companies of riflemen (Captain Willoughby Morgan's and Captain Joseph Kean's), *a half company* (Captain Benjamin K. Pierce's) *of artillery, under the command of Colonel Anthony Butler.*[4]

This is the first reference to Benjamin K. Pierce's association with Michigan. Unfortunately, however, he was not present at the historic event of July 18 on Mackinac Island; he was still on duty at Fort Pike, Sackett's Harbor, Lake Ontario. The half-company of Pierce's artillery command was on detached service to the Detroit Fifth Military District and was selected to accompany Colonel Butler to Mackinac.

In the possession of the New Hampshire Historical Society are the Army Orderly Books of Pierce's brother-in-law, General John McNeil. The entries in those books begin with the late spring of 1813 at Fort Pike and continue through the period during which General McNeil was stationed at Mackinac Island and was commandant of Fort Mackinac.

The McNeil Orderly Books show Captain B. K. Pierce stationed at Fort Pike from

19

June 25 through July 4, 1815, on which day he was Officer-Of-The-Day; the troops reviewed; and a salute "in honor of the day" was fired. On July 6, 1815, is this entry: "Dept 5 (Gen. Macomb's Detroit Headquarters) Michilimackinac — Captain B. K. Pierce . . . All Captains without loss of time will proceed to the posts and places to which they are assigned, General Brown, Comdg."

Despite the order to proceed "without loss of time," Captain Pierce officiated at a court martial hearing at Fort Pike on July 11, was Officer-Of-The-Day, July 12, through July 18, the day his detached half-company participated again in raising the Stars and Stripes over Fort Mackinac, 1,000 miles from Fort Pike.

The first definite proof of Pierce's presence in Michigan is a lengthy orderly book entry, in Pierce's handwriting:

Headquarters — Dept. 5 — Detroit — Aug. 13, 1815, — The Brig. Gen. has been informed that the soldiers are in the habit of milking the cows of the inhabitants. To prevent improprieties of this kind, the most rigorous discipline must be enforced and the slightest depredations punished with exemplary severity.

Following further instructions, the entry closes with:

The standing orders of the Post will remain in force until countermanded. The morning reports will be made agreeable to the form prescribed by the Act'g Brig-Major. By Order - B. K. Pierce, Captain Art'y.

This August 13, 1815, entry indicates that Pierce, at the time, was functioning in a higher rank than Captain of a company, possibly as Aide or Adjutant to the officer in overall command. There were several Generals, Colonels, and Majors at Detroit in August, 1815. The phraseology of Pierce's order affords an excellent insight into the character of the man as an officer. His order was definite and explicit. It spoke with authority and was to be obeyed.

According to "Garrison Orders — Mackinac, August 28, 1815: Brevet Lt. Col. Chambers of the rifle company assumes command of this post." This is followed by an August 29 entry: "Captain Pierce, of the Artillery, will select from Lt. Morgan's command as many men as may be required to complete his Company." Captain Pierce had rejoined his half-company on Mackinac Island, and this was to be the scene of his military activities for the next six years.

The remaining months of 1815 were devoted to routine military duties. For Christmas, Captain Pierce issued extra rations of liquor to his command and an exemption of one tour of duty for the first, second, and third best-appearing musket in the Christmas parade. "The worst shall have his liquor stopped for one month."

No reference has been found regarding the holiday social activities of Fort Mackinac's officers among the small but aristocratic society of the Island. However, handsome army officers, particularly at the age of twenty-six, have an attraction all their own; so, in the military orderly book this logical and inevitable entry:

> *Company Orders - Ft. Mackinac, April 3, 1816 — The Captain, having been married last evening, presents his Company with eight gallons of whiskey to drink to his health in commemoration of the event. B. K. Pierce, Captain Art'y.*

The bride was Josephine (Josette) La Framboise, age twenty-one, daughter of wealthy and prominent Mackinac fur-traders. Josette was born on the Island, September 24, 1795, when Mackinac was a British possession. In 1809, her father, of French descent, while kneeling in prayer one evening at one of his outposts, was shot and killed by an Indian who had asked for whiskey and had been refused.

The bride's mother, Marguerite Madgeline, was the daughter of Jean Baptiste Marcot (French) and Marie Neskesh, who "was of chiefly blood, being the daughter of Kewi-Na-Quot, one of the most powerful chiefs of the Ottawa Indian tribe." Madame La Framboise was "a remarkable woman in many ways . . . spoke French easily . . . a graceful and refined person, remarkably entertaining. She always wore the full Indian costume, and there was at that time no better fur-trader than she."

Such, briefly, was the family background of Josephine La Framboise "whom Capt. Pierce addressed and married . . . a highly educated and cultivated woman. Her graceful demeanor was a charm. She was small in person, a clear brunette with black eyes and very black hair." At the time of her father's death, Josephine, age fourteen, was being educated in a convent at Montreal, Canada. Her mother continued this practice in the following years, which accounts, no doubt, for Captain Pierce's bride's being highly educated and cultured.

The picture of Captain Pierce used in this biography is from an oil painting by an officer stationed at Mackinac Island, and undoubtedly is a wedding portrait. A picture of the bride was also painted, but so far it has not been located.

An interesting sidelight to Benjamin K. Pierce's marriage was located in *Early Days On Mackinac Island:*

> *This marriage took place at the home of a great friend of the young lady's (Josephine). In May, 1817 . . . Madame La Framboise arrived in Mackinac by bateau (Mackinaw boat) with her furs. She then hired a birch-bark canoe and Indian crew to take her to Montreal, where she went to place her boy in school. Her daughter was to be married that summer, but had to await her mother's return. As soon as the mother did return, the wedding took place. As Madame could not have time to open her house and make preparations at that late date, the home of Mrs. Mitchell . . . was insisted upon, by her whole family, as being the place for the wedding. The friendship between the families was sincere, and in this home, famed for its handsome weddings, another was added to the list.[5]*

Thus, it appears there were two wedding ceremonies, not an unusual event of that period. The April 2, 1816, ceremony took place in the absence of the bride's mother and the summer ceremony was during the time that Madame La Framboise was present on the Island. It was her custom to conduct winter fur-trading activities at her post 300 miles southwest of Mackinac Island, the site of the present city of Grand Rapids, Michigan. She returned to the Island only two or three months of the year, usually May through July.

During the period between Captain Pierce's first arrival at Mackinac in August, 1815, through the Christmas-New Year holiday season to April 2, 1816, Pierce had eight months in the tight, elite, little social circle of the Island to meet and court Josephine La Framboise "whom he addressed and married," the eventual and inevitable result when two (Pierce, age 26 and Josephine, age 21) "handsome, cultured, highly educated" personalities meet.

As there were no priests, ministers, or churches on Mackinac Island at the time, the wedding must have been a civil one, performed by Pierce's commanding officer, Colonel Talbot Chambers, or perhaps by Major William H. Puthoff, who was appointed Mackinac justice of the peace in 1815, following his retirement from the army at Detroit. This civil ceremony accounts for the second or summer ceremony as detailed in *Early Days.*

According to the custom among the more substantial and particularly the Catholic French families, marriages were strictly formal and solemn, performed according to church ritual. Upon her return to Mackinac in May, 1816, the bride's mother, "a devoted Catholic," apparently desired (or possibly it was previously agreed upon by Pierce and Josephine) to follow custom and solemnize the marriage, which, in the absence of a priest, was performed by a "marguillier" or layman of Catholic faith who was "firmly bound to administer the affairs of the church as his own, upon his soul and conscience."

The *Early Days* account closes with:

To this wedding, none but the officers and families of the garrison, and only two families of the town, were invited. The mother and aunt, Madame Schindler, were present in full Indian costume. After the marriage, the captain took his wife to the fort and Madame La Framboise departed to resume her work.

Josephine's mother's departure was, according to custom, the return to her southern Michigan trading post, which normally occurred following the annual June-July rendezvous of fur-traders.

The summer wedding of Captain Pierce and Josephine must have presented a picturesque scene with the officers of Fort Mackinac attending in their ornate uniforms of the period, enhanced by the dress of their wives. One must add the novel appearance of the bride's mother and aunt " in full Indian costume." Whether the bride was similarly attired was not recorded; however, from accounts of other Mackinac Island marriages of the same

FORT MACKINAC. CIRCA 1815–1818.

period, it appears such Indian dress for the bride was customary. The best man for Captain Pierce was, most likely, his younger brother, Lieutenant John Sullivan Pierce, likewise stationed at Mackinac.,

Typical of the situation on the Island, Pierce's bride, born September 24, 1795, was not given the ceremony of baptism until July 7, 1799, at age 4, when the famed Father Gabriel Richard, of Detroit, made a summer voyage to the Island that year.[6]

Difficult to account for is the absence in the Pierce family correspondence of any letter or reference to this first marriage of Benjamin K. Pierce, despite the fact that letters and references to his later two marriages are available. Pierce wrote his father at the time of his second (Amanda Boykin) marriage, and it is logical to assume he informed his family of his first marriage; the births of his daughter, Harriet, and his son, Langdon; and the deaths of Josephine and son. Somewhere, perhaps, such documents exist among the descendants of Harriet. Fortunately, *Early Days on Mackinac Island* supplies the missing information.

There are two errors in *Early Days:* "The second wedding ceremony took place in 1817." It should read "1816" on the basis of Pierce's Orderly Book entry. Also, "Mrs. Pierce did not live long. She died in 1821." According to the Pierce-La Framboise tomb inscription in Mackinac, Josephine died November 24, 1820. Mrs. Baird recorded her "Memiors" at an advanced age and long after she had departed from the Island, which accounts for the discrepancy in dates.

VI MACKINAC ISLAND
1816-1818

The McNeil Orderly Books are replete with many bits of information about Captain Benjamin K. Pierce's tour of duty on Mackinac Island. Brevity permits only mention of highlights.

On May 12, 1816, Captain Pierce, Chief of Artillery, was placed in charge of Fort Holmes, situated on a hilltop overlooking Fort Mackinac, with orders "to put into the most effective state of defense which his means will admit of" in expectation that "an attack by the British or Indians during the ensuing summer is not impossible."

On August 1–10, 1816, Captain Pierce, with units of his command, was at "the mouth of the Fox River" in Wisconsin with orders to support other troops in a landing operation to erect Fort Howard. This site was in the heart of the Winnebago-Menominee Indian country and the offensive, warring Outgami (Fox) tribe. The anticipated Indian attack did not materialize; consequently, this August 10 order: "Captain Pierce's detachment of artillery will return to Mackinac on board the vessels now here."

Accompanying the expedition was Major Charles Gratiot, United States Corps of Engineers, "to select a suitable position to fortify." Major Gratiot, of another prominent pioneer Detroit family, eventually became General Gratiot, Chief Engineer of the United States Army. In later years, Pierce served an interesting short period on detached, special duty with Gratiot's Corps of Engineers.

On October 15, 1816, Brevet Lieutenant Colonel John McNeil, Pierce's brother-in-law, assumed command of Fort Mackinac and the surrounding country. With McNeil's arrival there were three members of the Pierce family on the Island: Benjamin K., his half-sister, Elizabeth, and his younger brother, Lieutenant John Sullivan Pierce.

According to the Pierce family genealogical records, a son, John Winfield Scott, was born to the McNeils on Mackinac Island, February 17, 1817. Twenty years later he died a hero in a battle with Florida's Seminole Indians. In the same year, Captain Pierce and his

25

wife, Josephine, became the parents of a daughter, Harriet. The exact date in unrecorded. There were no churches, priests, or ministers on the Island at that period, and births remained unrecorded.

Because of the poor health of McNeil and his consequent absence, Captain Pierce was placed in temporary command of Fort Mackinac, June 1–15, 1817; again on July 22; and finally, upon the transfer of Colonel McNeil to Fort Gratiot (60 miles north of Detroit), on September 21, 1817,

> *Agreeable to the order of Colonel McNeil (and obviously with the approval of General Macomb) of this date, Captain B. K. Pierce of the Corps of Artillery, assumes the command of the Post of Michilimackinac.*

Thus, at the age of twenty-seven, Our Worthy Commander became the commandant of the strategic and important Great Lakes military post of Fort Mackinac.

During the winter of 1817–18 there was a shortage of firewood on Mackinac Island, and the troops were in need of shoes and winter clothing. Pierce solved those problems by having wood cut on a nearby (Bois Blanc) island and hauled to Mackinac by sleigh over the frozen waters. Leather was purchased from the Indian agent and made into shoes, while blankets were obtained from the trading posts and converted into clothing.

Except for the wood, shoes, and clothing problems (plus routine entries for the balance of the year 1817, and the first few months of 1818) the McNeil Orderly Books cease to be a Pierce reference source. After March, 1818, all further entries are "Fort Gratiot." Other sources, however, furnish interesting information.

On December 24, 1819, the *Detroit Gazette* reviewed a series of lectures given by a Major Whiting at the Detroit Lyceum, entitled: "Report On The Upper Lakes." Whiting referred to Saginaw Bay (100 miles north of Detroit) as:

> *. . . about 30 miles wide at its mouth, and 50 or 60 miles deep, receiving at its (western) end a large river bearing the same name, the length and dimensions of which have never yet been accurately ascertained. Captain Pierce of the army who crossed it in the winter of 1818–19, in coming from Mackinac to Detroit, and who explored it to the height of about 20 miles, reports it to be a considerable river, both as to width and depth, and the soil on both sides, so far as could be judged by appearances during the winter, to be excellent.*

With the military headquarters at Detroit, and as commandant of Fort Mackinac, Pierce apparently made frequent business trips between the two points using sailboat in the summer and snow shoes or dog sled in the winter.

Whether Captain Pierce's exploration of the Saginaw Bay country had any influence on it, the fact remains that in 1822 General Macomb ordered a detachment of the Third United States Infantry Regiment to the Saginaw River where the troops erected a stockade fort in the present city of Saginaw to control the Chippewa Indians who had become "restless and ill-tempered."

In the research for a series of newspaper articles on the founding of Birmingham, Michigan (twenty-five miles north of Detroit), it was noted that the name Pierce (and Pierce Street) was associated with other "first land purchasers" of what was then a wilderness forest, merely an Indian camping site where a small trail crossed the River Rouge. Research in the Lands Department, National Archives, Washington, D.C., disclosed that a "Benjamin K. Pierce, of Michilimackinac, on the 30th of December 1818, purchased . . . at Detroit . . . 160 acres . . . for $320 ($2 per acre), . . . with $80 down payment," a quarter section of land in what is today part of the main business district of the city of Birmingham.

There are several circumstances which most likely influenced Captain Pierce to make that purchase: the recollection of his father's wilderness land purchase in New Hampshire, which became his home; the possibility that Pierce, married and with a family, contemplated retiring from the military; or as an investment, perhaps, advised by General Macomb, from a family of large land holdings. Most important, no doubt, was the feverish land speculation rampant in Detroit at that period. Whatever his reason, his career as a soldier and unforeseen developments thwarted whatever objective he had in mind. Although his land was never cleared while in his possession, nor did he reside on it, he referred to it as "his farm" and visited it at every opportunity.

La Framboise Chateau on Mackinac Island.
Built by Captain Pierce for his family in 1820.

VII   MACKINAC ISLAND
1818-1820

There is a more or less blank period in the military career of Benjamin K. Pierce in the period from mid-1818 to 1820. A clerk of the American Fur Company visited Mackinac Island in June, 1818 and recorded a word picture of Captain Pierce's surroundings:

The island was then in its gayest season. All the traders attached to the American Fur Company were assembled there, having brought in their furs, and were preparing to receive their outfits to depart again to their several posts. The resident population of the island was about 500, principally Canadian, French, and mixed Indian-French; their occupation was fishing and trading with the Indians; with few exceptions they were poor and improvident.

According to the clerk's narrative: "there was a garrison of about three companies." Pierce's mother-in-law, Madame La Framboise, was one of the American Fur Organization's most successful and wealthy traders.

Fort Mackinac was situated on a high bluff overlooking the Village. For more than a century Mackinac Island had been the focal point for the Indian fur trade and a vital military post under French, British, and American domination. Captain Pierce frequently encountered considerable difficulty in controlling his troops who had a fondness for fur-trader's liquor and Indian tepees. Today Mackinac Island and its famous "Hill of History" is a popular summer tourist attraction, with the fort and adjacent buildings of Pierce's time restored and well maintained.

Whether the Pierce family resided in quarters within the fort, or in the home of his mother-in-law, or some other residence is not clearly recorded. Whatever the previous abode, apparently early in 1820, the family moved into a newly constructed La Framboise house "which Captain Pierce had, with her money, built for her," according to the Baird Memoirs.[7]

The La Framboise Chateau, sometimes referred to as the Pierce House, is still standing, well maintained and occupied. It was built on a tract of bayshore land owned by Madame La Framboise by Patent of the United States, dated July 3, 1812. Succeeding owners, following the death of Madame La Framboise on April 11, 1846, have added living quarters at the rear, and a veranda with Grecian columns at the front, creating an imposing structure which has been featured in various publications under the title, "Famous American Homes."

Every reference source thus far uncovered appears to justify the conjecture that in that house Langdon, the first son of Benjamin K. Pierce, was born and died. Records also indicate that in the La Framboise Chateau, the winsome brunette bride of April, 1816, Josephine, wife of Captain Pierce, died on November 24, 1820, and the age of 25. Burial of Josephine and son Langdon was in a plot of land adjacent to the home, donated by Josephine's mother not only for the burial, but for a church site. Today, the remains, including those of Madame La Framboise, are in an above ground sepulcher at the entrance to St. Anne's Catholic Church on Mackinac Island.

From the Baird Memoirs: "Mrs. Pierce did not live long. She died in 1821 (1820) leaving two children. The son did not long survive the mother." In interviews with the older residents of Mackinac Island, the general consensus was that "the wife of Captain Pierce died in childbirth."

Thus, there is recorded the first of several tragic events in the life of Our Worthy Commander: the loss of his wife and first born son, and no mother for his three year old daughter. As it was the custom of Madame La Framboise, in the pursuit of her fur-trading business, to winter at her lower Michigan trading post, Pierce temporarily placed his daughter in the care of his sister Elizabeth, wife of General McNeil, at Fort Gratiot.

Doctor William Beaumont, surgeon and War of 1812 veteran, arrived at Mackinac Island, via Detroit, on June 16, 1820. Doctor Beaumont was destined to attain international fame for his experiments at Mackinac on the chemical nature of the digestive process in the human body. In his diary he recorded: "June 17, dined with Captain Pierce; June 18, assumed charge of the hospital . . . obtained two horses of Captain Pierce and procured a private waiter on the 20th Inst."

On November 1, Doctor Beaumont wrote a lengthy letter to United States Medical Headquarters, Washington, D.C., on behalf of Pierce. It appears General Macomb has granted a portion of public gardens within the Mackinac military reservation for the erection of buildings to be used by the Indian Department. Captain Pierce, as commandant, had previously refused the Indian agent permission to use the land, but was overruled by his superior, General Macomb, at Detroit. From the Beaumont letter:

Impelled by a sense of duty, as well as feelings of justice and humanity towards the sick under my charge. I cannot withhold an exhibition of this (Macomb) order . . . . Capt. Pierce, actuated by purely patriotic motives and principles of justice to his command, refused his (Indian Agent, George Boyd) request, explicitly stated to him as his reasons that there was not ground enough in the whole public gardens to furnish the necessary vegetables for the use of the troops of this garrison . . . . Notwithstanding this (Pierce's refusal) he (Boyd) persisted in his unreasonable application until through some undue influence . . . the (Gen. Macomb's) order had been inconsideratley granted, regardless of the opinions, feelings, comfort or convenience of the officers or the garrison.

Doctor Beaumont detailed the importance of the garden grounds as a source of medicinal herbs for the sick and invalid soldiers, closing with the statement:

I presume, Sir, you will readily form an idea of our wants and privations on this isolated, barren isle . . . and will duly appreciate our condition and redress our grievances. Humanity requires it from the Medical Department, and Justice demands it from the Nation.

Doctor Beaumont won his case and Captain Pierce's also. The Indian Agency buildings were built 300 feet east of the gardens.

This Beaumont letter is another excellent insight into the character of Benjamin K. Pierce. When faced with a problem concerning the welfare of the men under his command, he had the courage to resist higher echelons; namely, General Macomb, and incidentally, Lewis Cass, Governor of Michigan Territory, and ex-officio Superintendant of Indian Affiars, who, it is quite obvious, was the "undue influence" on General Macomb's order. Lewis Cass became Secretary of War (1831–36). Both Cass and Macomb were important officials in directing Florida's Second Seminole War.

As the only physician on the Island, as a surgeon to the troops, Doctor Beaumont was, beyond a doubt, in attendance a few weeks later at the birth of Pierce's son, at the death of his wife, and the eventual passing of newborn Langdon. The son was named after Governor Langdon of New Hampshire, Pierce's home state.

In the McNeil Orderly Books there are a great number of entries showing Pierce's ability as a worthy commander at Fort Mackinac: the care he took of the post, his training of the troops, and the general precautions he undertook to protect the property entrusted to him. Although a strict disciplinarian, he had an excellent understanding of human nature, and on frequent occasions praised his troops for their fine appearance and conduct, rewarding them with extra rations of liquor and opportunities for relaxation. Mackinac Island, at best, was a lonesome outpost, particularly during the winter when it was surrounded by ice four to five months of the year.

Pierce's efficiency as a military leader was noted during Florida's Seminole war when

Governor Call, in a confidential letter to President Jackson, praised the ability of Pierce in contrast to his other field officers "who were inefficient."

The final Pierce entry in the Beaumont diary is dated August, 1821. He left Mackinac Island, August 9, at 4 p.m.:

> *Fair wind, fine weather. . . . arrived at Detroit at 10 a.m. on the 12th. Rode 20 miles into the country with Captain Pierce to view his land in Oakland county. Returned next morning.*

It appears that the overnight trip on horseback was an attempt by Pierce to interest Doctor Beaumont in purchasing his 160 acres of land. Captain Pierce at that time had orders to report to Pensacola, Florida. He may have accompanied Doctor Beaumont to Detroit where Pierce was to terminate his Michigan military and personal affairs at that point. Whatever the purpose, Doctor Beaumont did not purchase. His thoughts were of Plattsburg and his forthcoming marriage to his "beloved" Deborah Platt Grum.

No. 9

Land Office at _Detroit_ _Mis Ty_
_9th_ day of _June_ 18_24_.

IT IS HEREBY CERTIFIED, That pursuant to several acts of Congress, providing for the sale of Lands of the United States, _Benjamin H. Pierce_ _____ of _Michilimackinac_ _____
on the _Thirtieth_ day of _December_ 1818 purchased of the Register of the Land Office at _Detroit_
the _North West quarter_ of the lot or section, numbered _Thirty six_ in township No. _Two_ _____ of the
Tenth _____ range of the _Detroit_ _____ district, containing _One hundred and sixty_ _____ acres,
(_North_) _____ at the rate of _Two_ _____ dollars and _____ cents per acre, for which _N W ¼_
section _____ the said _Benjamin H. Pierce_ _____ has made full payment, his account therefor being finally
settled and closed in the books of this office, as will appear by the following statement thereof, viz.

1819	DEBT		1819 1820	CREDIT		
Janry 28	To amt of the purchase money of said N.W.¼ Section	320	Janry 25 June 9	By amt of the first Instalment discount at 8 per cent per annum for 203 days on eighty dollars being amt of the 2nd Instalment		8 00 5 55
				do do for 1 year 203 days on do being the amt of the 3rd Instalment		9 95
				do do for 2 year 203 days on do being the amt of the 4th Instalment		16 55
				Cash in full		210 15
	Amt	320		Amt	320	

NOW, THEREFORE, BE IT KNOWN, That on presenting this certificate to the Commissioner of the General Land Office _Amt_ _320_
the said _Benjamin H. Pierce_ _____
shall be entitled to receive a patent for the lot or _N W ¼ of_ section above described,

Peter Audrain
Register of the Land Office.

Original land deed for Pierce's Birmingham, Michigan, property. He referred to the land as "his farm".

FORT SAN CARLOS DE BARRANCAS, PENSACOLA, FLORIDA
Captain Pierce was assigned to Pensacola with the Fourth Artillery Regiment in 1821.

VIII FORT SAN CARLOS
DE BARRANCAS
PENSACOLA,
FLORIDA

Following ratification of the treaty signed February 22, 1819, whereby the United States purchased Florida from Spain, formal possession ceremonies took place on July 21, 1821, at Pensacola, and a new era began in the life of Benjamin K. Pierce. To protect the new land and the many miles of gulf coastline, there was a major change in army organization and many units were reassigned.

On March 21, 1821, Pierce's former Corps of Artillery ceased to exist. From it were formed four regiments of artillery. In a general order issued May 17, 1821, the Fourth Regiment was assigned to Pensacola, Florida. Among the officers listed for duty with the Fourth Regiment was Captain Benjamin K. Pierce, to command Company D. On June 21, while still stationed at Mackinac Island, Pierce was officially transferred to his new unit, with Colonel Fenwick in command of the regiment and General Edmund P. Gaines in overall command of the Pensacola troops.

Although Pierce's Pensacola orders were dated May 17, his special duties as commandant at Mackinac apparently did not permit him to leave Michigan immediately. In the newspaper *Floridian,* a number of letters for B. K. Pierce were listed as being on hand at the local post office.[8] From that source of information, Pierce did not join his Pensacola command until late fall of 1821.

Captain Pierce's new post was the ancient Spanish fort, San Carlos De Barrancas and the newer Fort Barrancas, 1,500 miles south of his former Mackinac Island command, and was far different in atmosphere and climate. Both of the ancient Spanish forts are today well preserved sites on the grounds "aboard" Pensacola's United States Navy and Aviation Center.

Only vague details are known of Pierce's tour of duty at Pensacola. References in the *Floridian* indicate considerable activity by units of the Fourth Artillery Regiment in the area of Mobile Point, Alabama, which seems to coincide with President Monroe's message to

35

Congress on the importance of establishing a post at Mobile Point for the protection of New Orleans.

Whatever Captain Pierce's role in those activities was, a letter to his father at Hillsborough, dated June 9, 1823, from Shasta, Alabama, best explains the highlight of his Pensacola tour of duty:

My dear Father: You will no doubt be surprised, but I hope not disappointed or dissatisfied, at the news of my being married. Upon every view of the subject and after mature reflection, I found that my own prospects of happiness and respectability would both be brightened by a matrimonial connexion with a female of my choice.

On a visit to a gentleman's house in the state of Alabama, I became acquainted with a young lady, Miss Amanda Boykin, with whose reputation, deportment, and manners I was pleased, and I commenced addressing her.

We were married last evening. I am extremely anxious to visit you, and under the blessings of Providence, I hope and calculate to see you next season, accompanied by Mrs. Pierce.

Mrs. Pierce's friends are wealthy and highly respectable. My connexion with her meets the unqualified approbation of Colonel Fenwick and all my military friends, several of whom have accompanied me here by invitation.

I shall probably return to Barrancas towards the last of this month. Give my duty to my mother, my love to brothers and sisters, and receive the same from your affectionate son. B. K. Pierce

Thus, at the age of thirty-three, and three years following the death of his first wife, Josephine La Framboise, Captain Pierce remarried, and in the course of time his daughter, Harriet, acquired a half-brother, Benjamin (who would be Benjamin IV), and three half-sisters, Elizabeth, Amanda, and Charlotte.

The Boykin family, it appears, was of Welsh descent (Caernarvonvshire, Wales) and prominent in Alabama, Virginia, and South Carolona. Many "Boykins" reside in the south today, and are considered among the first families.

On October 1, 1823, Captain Pierce was promoted to Brevet-Major "for 10 years of faithful service in one grade," a more or less honorary rank permitting higher ration and expense allowances, but no increase in salary.

IX   FORT DELAWARE

An important source of information on Pierce's activities for the next few years are the *American State Papers* from which source is this entry: "B. K. Pierce, commanding at Norfolk, Virginia, 1824."[9] Consequently, within a year of his marriage to Amanda Boykin and as he had hoped in his June, 1823, letter to his father, Major Pierce had obtained a new assignment which terminated his tour of duty at Fort Barrancas, Pensacola.

Lieutenant John Sullivan Pierce, younger brother of Benjamin K. and associate in the War of 1812 and at Mackinac Island, died at Detroit, Michigan, September 28, 1824, age 28, leaving a wife and two children.

Fuel and other expenses listed for Major B. K. Pierce in *Military Affairs* show he was stationed at Fortress Monroe (Old Point Comfort) in 1825. On May 1, 1827, at a United States Marshall's auction, Pierce purchased a house and lot at St. Augustine, Florida, for five hundred and fifteen dollars. About a month later he sold it to a local physician, Doctor William Simmons, for one thousand four hundred dollars. Known today as the Fernandez-Llambias House, its history dates back to Don Pedro Fernando, 1784. Now in the hands of the local historical society, it has been restored, refurnished, and is open to the public as one of the historical attractions of the city. (Address: 31 St. Francis Street.)

In a "Statement of Allowances Made to the Officers of the Army for 1828" *(Military Affairs)* there are several notations about costs of transporting baggage, traveling expenses, and per diem allowances for Major B. K. Pierce "assigned to court martial duties." Presumably on a similar assignment he purchased the St. Augustine house.

The Army Register for 1829 shows "Brevet Major Pierce, permanent commander of Fort Delaware, post office New Castle."[10] At that post two more tragic events occurred in the life of Our Worthy Commander. One of them was the death of his second wife, Amanda Boykin.

It appears his wife died late in January, 1831 — possibly the 26th, 27th or 28th — because on February 11, Pierce replied to a letter from his father:

> *I rec'd yours dated Jan'y 31st (not located) and Brother Franklin's on the other side of the same sheet acknowledgeing the receipt of mine announcing the decease of my dear beloved Amanda.*

> *On this occasion my cup of grief and troubles seemed to be full and as much as human nature could bear, but the ice in the (Delaware) river prevented my carrying the dear remains to New Castle, and before an opportunity presented, a most tremendous calamity has befallen my command, as you will discover by the enclosed communication.*

> *I have this day (February 11) paid the last sad duties to my dear departed wife. I was enabled yesterday to get to New Castle, with all my children, and today the funeral took place at 12 o'clock in Episcopal Church with all due ceremony in the presence of a vast and respectable concourse of people.*

Fort Delaware was situated on an island below New Castle, hence the problem of ice. The tremendous calamity which has "befallen my command" was the accidental destruction of Fort Delaware by fire on the night of February 8:

> *. . . a night of the utmost anxiety and most labour that I ever did or perhaps ever could perform again.*

> *. . . the remains of my dear Amanda was deposited in one of the magazines, the doors and wooden work of which caught fire, and expecting that the coffin and body would be burnt, I took four men and rushed through a solid sheet of fire and brought it out on the center of the parade (grounds) where it was preserved.*

> *. . . my little children all the time in my quarters on the parade, I had determined to preserve them or perish with them. I directed some of my old soldiers and bravest men to ascend the roof of my house and by passing water to them and keeping the roof covered as with a heavy rain for nine hours without cessation, I succeeded in saving it from the flames, I sent the children and nurses into the kitchen and visited them about every half hour and encouraged them to be quiet and not be alarmed.*

> *The crashing of the falling timbers, the bright flames streaming to the skies and the interspersed thundering explosions of the powder that had been thrown outside presented a scene awfully sublime, but for me it presented neither attraction, nor terror - neither splendour, magnificence nor awe, I saw . . . that we had a herculean task before us and conducted myself accordingly, encouraging and rousing the men to continue, and as the danger pressed, to increase exertion.*

At the close of the letter Pierce stated: "Harriet and the four little children are very well as regards bodily health" but apparently disturbed by the events which had occurred. "I have for the present left my children with my friend, Major Stacklow."

Following the fire, Major Pierce demanded a Court of Inquiry "to inquire into the causes and circumstances" which led to the burning of Fort Delaware. Following a lengthy hearing:

> *The Court is unanimously of the opinion that neither blame nor censure can attach to Major Pierce, the commandant, nor to any of his command. . . . the Court is in justice bound to express further opinion that much credit is due them for their zeal and perservering efforts to contend with the difficulties constantly opposing them, even to the sacrifice of their personal property and imminent danger to which their families were so long exposed.*

On September 8, 1831, a group of investigating army engineers reported "we are decidedly of the opinion that Fort Delaware is irreparable."[11]

At the age of 41, Major Benjamin K. Pierce was again a widower with a motherless family of five children: the oldest Harriet, age 14, from his first marriage; the four from his second marriage, in age from about seven to the youngest probably born in 1830. The cause of his beloved Amanda's death is undetermined.

Delaware City Feby 11th 1831

My Dear Father,

I recd. yours dated Jany 31st. & Brother Franks On the other side of the same sheet acknowledging the receipt of mine announcing the decease of my dear beloved Amanda — On this occasion my cup of grief & trouble, seemed to be full & as much as human nature could bear, but the ice in the river prevented my carrying the dear remains to New Castle & before an opportunity presented, a most tremendous calamity has befalen my command as you discover by the enclosed communication — I have this day paid the last sad duties to my dear departed wife — I was enabled yesterday

A portion of the letter written by Benjamin K. Pierce to his father while Benjamin K. Pierce was stationed in Delaware, 1831.

X SECOND FLORIDA
ASSIGNMENT:
FORT DEFIANCE

In a letter to his father, dated September 26, 1832, Pierce reported he had suffered a broken leg, with no details. Following an operation, "painful but necessary, . . . I believe, in a fair way of having at least a strong limb." Also, "from private and confidential intelligence" the troops under his command were to be moved to Washington or to some post in Virginia. He referred to an insurrection in the south and "it is the duty of the government to protect our southern brethren."

The insurrection referred to was, most probably, a slave uprising in Virginia led by Nat Turner, which resulted in considerable bloodshed. Virginia and North Carolina troops subdued the insurgents; consequently, northern troops were not required.

American State Papers disclose Pierce's activities following the Delaware fire. From New Castle he was assigned to Philadelphia, apparently on recruiting duty. During that period he made frequent journeys to Fort Hamilton, New York, and to Washington, D.C., where his brother, Franklin, was a representative in Congress from New Hampshire.

In the summer of 1833, under a statement of pay and allowances, there is recorded for Major Pierce:

> *From Fort Hamilton to Mackinac, on court-martial duty, 1,073 miles; thence to Fort Niagara, 663 miles; thence to Fort Hamilton, 466 miles, July and August, 1833; total 2,202 miles at 10¢ - $220.20 - plus a per diem allowance of $1.00 for 20 days at Mackinac and Niagara, and traveling to and from - $73.39.*

Detroit was a necessary stopover to the upper Great Lakes Mackinac country; therefore, it is entirely possible he visited his Birmingham, Oakland County, property on that journey.

On December 30, 1835, this report to the Commissary General of Subsistence, United States Army, by Joseph W. Harris, Lieutenant, District Agent, Florida Indians, was written from Fort King (Ocala):

41

I regret that it becomes my first duty after my arrival here . . . to relate to you . . . our excellent superintendent, General Wiley Thompson, has been most cruelly murdered by a party of hostile Indians and with him Lt. Constantine Smith, of the 2nd Regiment of Artillery; Erastus Rogers, the sutler of the post, together with his two clerks – a Mr. Hitzler and a boy called Robert. This occurred on the afternoon of the 28th instant, between three and four o'clock.

The cowardly murderers are supposed to be a party of the Mikasuki tribe of 40 or 60 strong under the traitor Powell (Osceola), whose shrill peculiar war whoop was recognized by our interpreter. . . . I am apprehensive that the hostile disposition is a very general one. All the upper (Florida) Indians with but a few exceptions . . . have gone over to the war party.[12]

On the same day, fifty miles south, the Dade massacre occurred. One hundred men from Company C, Second Artillery, and Company B, Third Artillery, plus eight officers under the command of Major Francis L. Dade were ambushed and annihilated under the leadership of three noted Indian chiefs: Micanopy, Alligator, and Jupiter. Only one member of the troops, Ransom Clarke, survived to record the details.

On the last day of 1835, 250 United States regulars, plus 500 Florida volunteers attempted to oust Osceola and his warriors from their hiding place in the swamps bordering the Withlacoochee River, but failed in their objective.

Thus, it was the start of the Second Seminole Indian War. Inevitably, Major Benjamin K. Pierce was assigned once again to Florida, but this time east to Florida's peninsula.

At the time of the Thompson-Dade episode, Pierce, with a detachment of the Fourth Artillery, was in command of Fort Lafayette, New York Harbor. In a letter to General McNeil, dated May 18, 1836, Franklin Pierce wrote: "Benjamin is looking fairly well and starts with his detachment tomorrow." His destination was St. Augustine. On August 15, he was ordered by Lieutenant Colonel Crane, commander of the Florida troops, to proceed to Fort Defiance (near Micanopy), with orders to close out the fort. He arrived five days later, August 20, with twenty-seven wagons of supplies and one hundred twenty-five troops.

Upon his arrival at Micanopy, Major Pierce made a decision which was to reward him with a citation for distinguished service, a promotion in rank, and wide acclaim in the north.

Ten miles south of Micanopy was the abandoned Fort Drane which had been deemed unsuitable from a strategic viewpoint because of the unusual amount of sickness at the post. The abandoned fort "was a favorite resort for the enemy, who congregated there to gather the sugar-cane and corn in the extensive fields planted by General Clinch the season previous." Pierce's decision was to immediately invade the area, an event best described by his own report to Lieutenant Colonel Crane:

Micanopy, August 21, 1836. Sire: I have the honor to report to you that I arrived here yesterday and learning that there were Indians lurking about Fort Drane, ten miles south of this post, I determined to make an expedition against them. For this purpose I marched at two o'clock this morning, with 110 men and a piece of ordnance . . .

I arrived at Fort Drane about sunrise, attacked the Indians, who proved to be numerous, say 300 Mikasuki Indians, commanded by Powell (Osceola). Lieutenants Irwin and Herbert on the right; Captain Childs and Lieutenant Spalding on the left; the artillery in the center, commanded by Lieutenant Pickell. All attacked with vigor and spirit, drove them three-fourths of a mile into an extensive hammock — and in a hurried passage over the field counted ten dead.

This engagement was well contested by the Indians, who fought with determined bravery for more than an hour. The recesses to which they retreated could not be penetrated by our exhausted and inferior force. I therefore marched the detachment back to Micanopy, leaving no killed or wounded on the field. Our loss was one dead and sixteen wounded . . . none thought dangerous. B. K. Pierce, Major Commanding.

Major Pierce's twenty-four years of military service through the War of 1812, and his later tour of duty in the Indian country of the Great Lakes proved to be valuable experience. His manner of attack was in the classic military plan found most effective in engagements with Indians; and early dawn surprise-rushing attack with an artillery piece protected on both sides.

In that particular engagement, Pierce mounted a portion of his artillery men on the horses used to haul his wagon train of supplies. The improvised cavalry galloped into the Indian camp. The Indians, who were "caught in the open, scurried into the edge of a hammock where they formed as much of a line as they ever did, and commenced to return a heavy fire. In reply, the white cannon rattled cannister in the palmettos."

From the beginning of the Second Seminole War, events had been decidedly in favor of Osceola's Seminoles and their allies; consequently, Pierce's successful attack was widely publicized as a favorable turn in the prosecution of the war.

In a letter to General McNeil about his brother's Florida tour of duty, Franklin wrote: "The manner in which his services are noticed in the Georgia and Florida papers show the estimation in which he is held in that section." He also quotes from one of the papers: "The two head chiefs, the most warlike and the most hostile, next to (Osceola), the one of the Mikasukis, the other of the Long Swamp tribe, were killed by Major Pierce at Fort Drane."

Floridians very much admired Pierce. Their admiration in itself, was no small compliment, for they were usually suspicious of the regular army. General Call wrote confidentially to the President (Jackson) that except for Pierce, his field officers were inefficient. Accordingly he wished a brevet colonelcy given Pierce so that he may outrank the lieutenant colonels who would otherwise command him. [13]

(Pierce's 24 years of service gave him seniority as a Lieutenant Colonel.)

Governor Call replied to Pierce's Fort Drane report:

Tallahassee, September 6, 1836. Sir, I have received through Colonel Crane a copy of your official report of the battle of Fort Drane. Your conduct and that of the officers and men under your command, on that occasion, reflects on you and upon them the highest credit. To have beaten Powell (Osceola) with one third of his force was a proud achievement; and I take this occasion to tender my acknowledgements to you and your command for this gallant service. I am, sire, very respectfully, your obedient servant. R. K. Call, Commander in Chief.

Call's commendation was followed by another from General Macomb:

Head-Quarters Of The Army, Adjt. General's Office – Washington, September 16, 1836. General order ♯61. ♯1. The Major General Commander in Chief has received the official account of the attack made on the 21st of August, by Maj. Pierce, of the First Regiment of Artillery, on a large body of Indians collected on the site of old Fort Drane, in which, with a force of only 110 men, he completely surprised and routed about 300 warriors, and killed and wounded a considerable number of them. ♯2. The conduct of officers and men engaged in this enterprise . . . is deserving of the highest praise. ♯3. It is with much satisfaction that the Major General recurs to the conduct on all occasions of the troops of the regular army who have been serving in Florida against the Seminoles. Wherever they have had an opportunity of meeting the enemy, they have acted with a spirit of gallantry . . . which reflects honor on the character of the American army, and entitles them to the approbation and regard of their government and country. By order of Major General Macomb. Major General Commander in Chief.

The Fort Drane battle was the first defeat suffered by the feared Osceola, and undoubtedly afforded some satisfaction to Major Pierce as a just retribution for the massacre of Major Dade and his detachment of artillery men. On October 21, 1836, Benjamin K. Pierce wrote a letter to his father which contained this closing statement: "The President has breveted me Lieutenant Colonel for what he terms 'Distinguished Services' at the Battle of Fort Drane."

Lieutenant Colonel Benjamin K. Pierce was, indeed, a "Worthy Commander."

Portion of a letter from Franklin Pierce to General McNeil, Hillsborough, New Hampshire, November 6, 1836.

XI   THE BATTLE OF
WAHOO SWAMP

The order Pierce received to close out Fort Defiance was part of a plan by Florida's Governor Richard K. Call for a campaign against the Seminoles. Less than a month after Pierce encountered Osceola at Fort Drane, Call left Tallahassee with a Tennessee volunteer brigade of 1,200 men and 140 Florida militia. Their destination was the Indian camp in the Cove of the Withlacoochee River, south of Lake Tsala Apopka. Pierce, at the time, was awaiting orders at Black Creek near Jacksonville.

After crossing the Suwanee River, General Call divided his army; on September 29, he dispatched a part of his forces, with ten days' rations, to Fort Drane, where they arrived October 1. Meanwhile, "the night before an express was sent to Major Pierce at Black Creek advising him of my intended movements, and directing him to advance without delay his forces and all the transport wagons and supplies for the army."

According to Call's report:

The express sent to Major Pierce did not, for some cause, arrive at Black Creek by three days as early as it should have done. But expecting my orders, his (Pierce's) wagons were all loaded and in readiness, and in two hours after the arrival of the express, though it was late at night, his whole train was in motion, and he joined me on the evening of the 8th of October.

That hurried march of Pierce and his troops gained him additional praise. Florida's papers admiringly noted that in order to expedite Call's campaign, Pierce had cut sixty-five miles of new road in five days with a battalion of 200 artillery men; "it is zeal and energy like this that the times require, and it is this that gains the confidence of the General in Chief and saves the army from want."

Pierce's arrival at Fort Drane raised Call's strength to approximately 1,350. Call and his troops proceeded to the Withlacoochee where they arrived on October 13. However, because of the withering fire of the Indians who were well ensconced in their cove on the opposite of the river, together with the shortage of supplies and the failure of co-ordination with other units, Call, "in this trying situation, . . . consulted with General Armstrong and

Major Pierce," and resolved to march back to Fort Drane. The troops arrived there on October 17.

One month later, on November 13, Call's troops, reinforced with a regiment of Creek Indians, were again at the Withlacoochee, but found the area abandoned. Dividing his forces, Call assigned to the now Lieutenant Colonel Pierce the duty of working his way south; both units, General Call's and Pierce's, were to meet at the scene of Dade's massacre near Bushnell, Florida.

On November 21, the reunited and combined force of approximately 2,500 men launched a concentrated attack on the opposing Indians in the Wahoo Swamp region south of the Withlacoochee River Cove. Pierce's participation in that battle is well described by his later report to Call:

> *Sir: Agreeable to your order of the night of the 20th instant, the troops under my command moved at early dawn on the 21st in search of the enemy (represented to be in large force in the Wahoo Swamp) in four separate columns and in the following order: Colonel Warren's command of mounted Floridians on the right; the battalion of artillery and a detachment of middle Florida volunteers, under Major Gardner, forming the second column; the third and fourth columns composed of Creek volunteers, commanded by Lt. Colonel Brown and Major Morris.*

After marching south about five miles and within 400 yards of the Wahoo Swamp, the enemy appeared in force at the edge of a hammock which skirted the swamp "and by their war-whoops and other indications showed themselves in readiness to give battle." Pierce's troops advanced in the arranged order, "opened a heavy fire," and gained the hammock:

> *I moved forward my whole division in pursuit of the enemy. Having pushed through an extensive swamp and hammock, driving the enemy before us for a distance of one and a half miles; a portion of our friendly (Creek) Indians at length reached a deep and difficult morass, on the opposite side of which the enemy were poised. In attempting the passage of this, Major Moniac was killed and sank in the stream.*
>
> *A sharp engagment then commenced on the part of our friendly Indians . . . the regular troops and Floridians were pushed forward as rapidly as possible to the scene of action but meeting with an almost insurmountable obstacle in a difficult miry swamp, half a mile in extent, and from two to three feet deep in mud and water, were prevented from reaching it, until one-half to three-quarters of an hour after the commencement of the engagement.*

Floundering through the waist high mud and water, Pierce's regulars reformed on higher ground, "opened a deadly fire at the enemy," and "at about half-past three o'clock p.m., the enemy's fire had nearly ceased."

From a continuation of his report to Governor Call, it appeared at that point in the battle that Pierce had two alternatives: to push on, or "return our killed and wounded to camp." Anxious to make the victory, so brilliant in its commencement, "complete in its termination and result," Pierce was inclined to further charge "at the point of bayonet." However, after consultation with his officers, it was decided to abandon the attempt because "of the exhausted state of the ammunition," the difficulty of the swampy terrain, and "the lateness of the hour, it being near night. . . . I then directed the killed and wounded to be brought to the front, formed a strong rear guard, and returned to the position occupied by your Excellency."

The losses in Pierce's command at the Battle of Wahoo Swamp were: Major Moniac and two Creek Indians killed; Captain Ross, United States Marine Corps, and three Creek Indians wounded. Of the artillery unit, five were killed, and Captain Maitland, two sergeants, two corporals and two privates wounded.

Following a lengthy commendation of officers and men, by name and unit, Pierce stated:

> *The perserverance in the difficulties of pursuit and the steadiness and courage in the battle, of the whole command, both officers and soldiers, throughout the day, cannot be too highly commended. . . . From the commencement of the action in the first hammock, to its close in the second, was nearly four hours. I think it a brilliant day, resounding to honor of our arms and calculated to bring the war to a speedy termination, I am Sir, with great respect, Your obedient servant, B. K. Pierce, Colonel Commanding Right Division.*

Such was the role of Benjamin K. Pierce, at the age of 46, in the Battle of Wahoo Swamp, November 21, 1836. It was a significant event in the Second Seminole War and the early history of Florida.

Vietnam veterans may recognize a similarity between their rice-paddy battles and that of Pierce's troops in the mud of Wahoo Swamp. Military analysts who state that the United States Army never before fought under such a type of guerilla warfare should review Florida's forgotten Second Seminole War all the way to the everglades.

Copy

St Augustine Oct 21, 1836

My Dear Father

I arrived here today on my way to
Savannah & Charleston on business by the appointment
of Govr Call Commander in chief of the Army in Florida.
I am in excellent health &c —

Savannah Georgia Oct 23, 1836

I arrived here this evening on my way to Charleston.
I leave here today, and expect to be in Charleston
tomorrow. I inclose Govr Calls order to me and a
column from the newspapers which will give
you a history of our late operations —

Charleston S.C. Tuesday 25th

Arrived here this Morning at day light
and before sunrise purchased three hundred
horses. I am in Excellent health and spirits. I
shall leave here for Gareys Ferry tomorrow having
done everything required and accomplished without
difficulty everything which I have attempted. Pray send
my love to my dear little children. The President has
brevetted me Lieut Colo for what he terms "distinguished
services at the battle of Ft Drane"

Give my love to all
In haste &c
Signed — B. K. Pierce

A letter written in 1836 by Benjamin K. Pierce to his father. Pierce was traveling north from Florida.

XII NORTHERN
ASSIGNMENT

At the time of the Wahoo Swamp battle, Pierce actually held three ranks as officer. In the United States Regular Army his official rank was Major, in addition to his status as Brevet Lieutenant Colonel. In the Wahoo Swamp report to Governor Call, he signed it, "B. K. Pierce, Colonel Commanding."

Technically, the troops engaged in the Wahoo Swamp affair were militia or volunteer civilians, augmented or supported by United States regulars (such as Pierce's artillery unit) and all were basically under the command of Governor Call. On October 21, 1836, the *St. Augustine Herald* carried this news item: "We are pleased to learn that Governor Call has conferred upon Major Pierce the appointment of Quartermaster General. We feel satisfied that the office could not be in better hands." With that assignment, Governor Call apparently conferred to Pierce the rank of full Colonel in the Florida militia. In the regular United States Army, Pierce was a line, field, and combat officer. In Call's Florida troops, he had a dual role: supply officer and field officer.

The *St. Augustine Herald* notice of Pierce's Quartermaster duties coincided with a letter Pierce dispatched to his father from St. Augustine, also dated October 21, in which he related, "I arrived here on my way to Savannah and Charleston on business by the appointment of Governor Call."

The business in which Pierce was involved is explained by the order he received:
To make the army to move with promptitude, 500 good fresh horses will be absolutely necessary. These you are authorized to purchase without delay. You will understand your instructions give you full authority to take any measure for the immediate and effectual prosecution of the campaign.

The wide and favorable publicity Pierce received in South Carolina and Georgia papers (". . . whose conduct in Florida has already excited the admiration of our readers, we hope that he will be successful in procuring all the material necessary for the prosecution of the war . . .") enabled Pierce to write his father from Charleston, October 25:

Arrived here this morning at daylight and before sunrise purchased 300 horses. I am in excellent health and spirit . . . having done everything required and accomplished without difficulty everything which I have attempted. Pray send my best to my little children.

One month later, Governor Call, with the newly acquired horses and supplies, launched his drive south. This resulted in Pierce's successful Wahoo Swamp battle. When Pierce's Right Division command was reunited with Governor Call's section, the troops moved sixty-five miles northeast to Volusia, where they arrived November 27. At Volusia, Governor Call received notice he had been relieved of his command, replaced by Brevet Major General Thomas S. Jesup, who, similar to Pierce, was a War of 1812 veteran. In the official return, "Troops Serving in Florida Under The Command of General Thomas S. Jesup For 1837," was this listing: Brevet Lieutenant Colonel B. K. Pierce, Major, First Artillery."

On January 1, 1837, General Jesup reported much sickness (malaria) prevailed among his Florida troops which reached epidemic proportions. Many army posts were abandoned, hospitals were established, and upon urgent recommendations by army surgeons, many invalids were sent north.

Among the ill was Benjamin K. Pierce. The main source of information on Pierce's activities in 1837 are fourteen letters written by his brother, Franklin, newly elected Senator from New Hampshire. Because of his illness, Pierce was ordered "to a northern climate." Consequently, he was at Charleston, South Carolina on January 22, and while there "mustered 300 South Carolina militia . . . he anticipated renewed fighting in the Indian country and has resolved to return to the seat of war although his health is not fully restored." On February 11, ". . . he was on the eve of leaving Savannah for Florida."

On February 28, Franklin wrote: "I received a letter yesterday from Benjamin, dated at Charleston on the 24th instant. His health is much improved. He has been ordered, at his request, to report himself to this city (Washington, D.C.)." This sudden change in Pierce's plans apparently was caused by several circumstances: he had received information that his father, age 80, "had a severe stroke of palsey" and that two sisters were severely ill. On April 7, Benjamin is to take command at Fort Hamilton." On April 8, "I expect to see him within a week. . . . I suppose he will be necessarily detained at Baltimore a few days as I understand Miss R. is now there." Miss R. was Louisa A. Read, who was destined to become the third Mrs. Benjamin K. Pierce.

While in New York at Fort Hamilton, Pierce received an assignment from General Charles Gratiot, Chief Engineer, United States Army, to inspect the military roads of Michigan. Michigan was no longer a territory; it was a state, admitted January 26, 1837.

As one of the roads to be inspected (Detroit to Saginaw) passed by his Birmingham, Oakland County, property, Pierce took advantage of the opportunity to inspect it. In a letter to General McNeil, dated July 26, 1837, Oakland County, Michigan, he wrote:

I have located myself here for a time on my farm . . . it is beautifully situated and is very valuable. . . . If I could remain here I could make thirty thousand dollars on it. . . . I was offered $200 today for an acre on the south side of my place. . . . This is a thriving village. . . . I have rode on horseback about 1000 miles, mostly on the different roads in the State and have nearly finished all my inspection. . . . I rather think I shall remain here until September and proceed by way of Hillsboro and Boston to Washington, etc., and thence I know not where.

At the conclusion of his letter Pierce wrote:

If it were not for this cursed war I would obtain a furlough or remain on duty here and to work upon my property which of my own interest almost imperatively requires, having devoted five and twenty years to the service of my country, I ought now to have a year or two to attend to my own concern by which time I could make myself independent.

Back at "Washington City, October 4, 1837," Pierce submitted a detailed report on the "Condition of (five roads) in Michigan" to General Gratiot, signed "B. K. Pierce, Lieutenant Colonel, United States Army on Engineer Service."[14]

Pierce returned from his Michigan tour of duty late in September. According to Senator Pierce, as of September 12, 1837: "Benjamin has not arrived here (Washington) though I heard of his arrival at New York as early as last Friday." Enclosed with the Senator's letter were details on "the sad intelligence" of Lieutenant John Winifield Scott McNeil's death, at the age of 20, in an engagement with the Seminole Indians south of St. Augustine, September 10. Lieutenant McNeil was the son of General John McNeil and his wife, Elizabeth (Pierce), born on Mackinac Island, February 17, 1817. Lieutenant McNeil was buried at St. Augustine "in holy ground and with those military honors which a gallant and honorable soldier should always receive from his bereaved comrades." That tribute was from Jacob R. Motte, the army surgeon who attended the young hero's wounds and who was present at his burial. While he was in Michigan, Pierce's sister, Nancy M., wife of General Solomon McNeil, died, August 27, at age forty-five.

Letter from Benjamin Pierce's brother, Franklin, to General John McNeil.
1837

XIII THIRD FLORDIA ASSIGNMENT: INDIAN RIVER INLET

If Lieutenant Colonel Benjamin K. Pierce had any doubts about his next assignment they were soon clarified upon his arrival in Washington. General Alexander Macomb, who recognized unusual abilities in Pierce twenty-five years previously in the War of 1812, ordered him back to Florida. Macomb, now Commander in Chief of the United States Army, was well acquainted with Pierce's service record. It is logical to assume Macomb believed the experience and ability of Pierce should be made available to General Jesup's well planned Florida winter campaign about to be launched. According to Senator Pierce, as of October 5 and 6, "Benjamin is here with me, occupying a room contiguous to mine, . . . I wish he could be excused from going to Florida again, but I suppose the department may think his services there important."

The exact date of Pierce's departure for the south is unrecorded, but his journey included a stopover at Baltimore, no doubt to see "Miss R.". He arrived at St. Augustine on November 19, 1837, where "he wept at the grave of our lamented Scott" (nephew Lieutenant McNeil). There he visited his former opponent, the famous Osceola (Powell), who was in irons in the Castilla de San Marco (Fort Marion). Osceola was seized one month earlier under a flag of truce.

Pierce left St. Augustine on the morning of November 22, and shortly after, Jacob R. Motte, army surgeon and recorder of events, reported: "Lieutenant Colonel Pierce arrived on the steamer Richmond from St. Augustine with the remaining companies of the First Artillery, accompanied by Major Kirby and other officers of the First Artillery. Many were fine young fellows just from the military academy at West Point." Up north, in Pierce's home country, another sister Harriet B. (Mrs. Hugh Jameson), died November 24, at thirty-seven. It was that sister for whom Benjamin K. Pierce's daughter, Harriet, now age twenty, was named.

History is indebted to Jacob R. Motte for his Journal in which he recorded for posterity the activities of Pierce on his third tour of duty in Florida. On November 29, "at daylight," the troops under the command of Lieutenant McLaughlin, in "about ten or a dozen

55

Mackinaw boats" departed "for a place called the 'Haulover'" about thirty miles south of Mosquito Inlet. General Hernandez "with the rest of his forces (including Pierce, apparently) intended following us to the designated place by land."

Motte states:

The site of our camp was an open prairie . . . of scrubsaw-palmetto . . . entirely bare of trees. One side, Indian River, . . . on the other side of us, the placid waters of Mosquito Lagoon . . . which may easily be found by looking at any map of Florida. On December 7, General Hernandez, with the cavalry, left us for the opposite side of Indian River.

With the departure of General Hernandez, Pierce was left in command of the remaining troops. According to Motte:

Colonel Pierce did not allow his regiment to be idle, but had them out every day for drills. In order to clear a sufficient space for drilling, the Colonel turned out the entire regiment and had the prairie set on fire on all sides. . . . I never beheld a more magnificent spectacle.

Colonel Pierce's troops celebrated Christmas Day, 1837, at the Haulover, that is, at Lieutenant Irwin's Fort Ann. Motte relates that "We revelled upon gopher soup and whiskey today, which were the chief luxuries which graced our board."

On December 28, Lieutenant Powell, commander of a navy detachment, sailed south on the Indian River "to select eligible sites for depots." On the eve of December 29, Colonel Pierce issued orders that the regiment "should be in readiness to embark at two in the morning. By daylight we were all aboard" and, as previously reported in Chapter Two, after quietly gliding all night down the river, they joined Lieutenant Powell at the Indian River Inlet on the afternoon of December 31. On January 2, the blockhouse of palmetto logs was erected and "dubbed Fort Pierce, after our worthy commander," Lieutenant Colonel Benjamin Kendrick Pierce, commander of the First Regiment of Artillery.

Motte noted the type of vessel Pierce used to transport the troops: "numerous large flat-bottomed boats, called Mackinaw boats . . . having been constructed expressly for the navigation of these shallow lagoons." This type of boat was the result, obviously, of Pierce's service in the Mackinac Island country of the northern Great Lakes. Mackinaw boats were noted for their sea worthiness and capacity for carrying large loads in relationship to their size.

Fort Pierce soon acquired a much higher status than merely the site of a blockhouse supply depot: "On the 14th January our remote and quiet little post presented quite a scene of bustle occasioned by the arrival of General Jesup and staff." General Jesup was accompanied by the Second Dragoon and 600 volunteers from Alabama and Tennessee.

With General Jesup's arrival, Fort Pierce became "Headquarters, Army of the South."

A Mackinaw Boat
Used by Pierce's troops in Florida.

This resulted in the first recorded official document referring to Fort Pierce other than Motte's Journal entry. From "Fort Pierce, January 15, 1838," Jesup issued an order to Brigadier General Hernandez: "General: Agreeable to your request, I have directed by the order of today, that you and the gentlemen of your staff, as well as the remainder of your brigade, be discharged from the service." Another official reference of January 15: "As it was important not only to communicate with General Taylor, but to be certain of supplies to Fort Pierce, I directed the troops to fall back . . . where they moved to Fort Pierce." Thus the area of Indian River Inlet was officially established as "Fort Pierce." It has managed, with a few narrow escapes, to retain this identification to the present time.

In concluding this brief history of Fort Pierce, mention should be made that the palmetto log blockhouse of Pierce's time was not the first fort established on "the bluff." Motte recorded:

> *The spot upon which we were encamped bore traces of having not long previous been the site of an Indian camp. ... The formation of the ground adjoining the bluff presented strong indications of its having been thrown up in a regular manner of fortification, but when, or by whom, will probably forever remain a secret; the antiquity only of its date made known by the enormous trees growing out of the embankments and entrenchments, which were easily to be distinguished.*

Motte's powers of observation were eventually verified by Yale University in a "Survey of Indian River Archeology." Two Spanish Jesuit missionary priests, Jose Maria Monaco and Jose Xavier de Alano, constructed a small fort on the bluff area during the first half of the eighteenth century. "The flag of Spain was raised on it on August 8, 1743," ninety-five years prior to Benjamin K. Pierce's appearance on the scene.

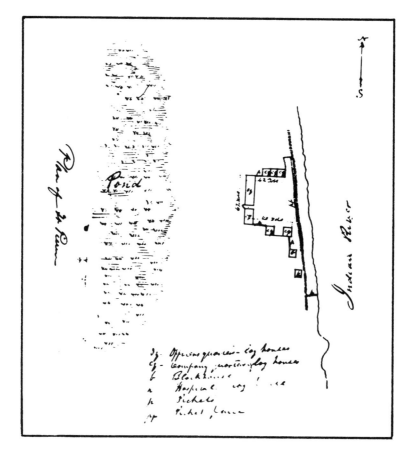

The original plan of Fort Pierce.
(From a copy in the Indian River Community College Historical Data Center.)

A replica of the palmetto log blockhouse dubbed Fort Pierce by Pierce's troops.

Actual area, about the size of a city block, was located one mile south of the St. Lucie County Courthouse on South Indian River Drive. (Courtesy of the St. Lucie County Historical Museum.)

Letters from B. K. Pierce to his brother Senator Franklin Pierce who later became President Pierce of United States

St. Augustine Jan'y 24th 1838

My dear Brother,

We have had a long & severe storm, which has prevented the Steam Boat from getting out of the Harbour, in which I had to take passage on my return to my Regiment & hence my detention has been unavoidable; as the storm still continues I do not know how many days more I may be delayed — News by express this moment reached here, that Lt Powell of the Navy, has had an engagement with the Indians on the St. Lucie River, & been woefully whipped — My Regiment I presume has marched before this to the scene of this battle & I regret exceedingly that I am absent but it is unavoidable — It is stated that Powell had about 120 men — 40 of whom were soldiers, & the remainder sailors — that himself & all his officers were wounded, that he left & some were obliged to be scalped, & one boat loaded with ammunition fell into the hands of the Indians — that the sailors fled at the first fire to their boats — Isn't this awful, following Col Taylor's action & this is almost a massacre — The forty Artillery with Lt Powell belonged to our Regiment, that the officers were nearly all killed & wounded & left upon the field — What an idea in sending a Naval officer on an exploring expedition, in time of War, with a hundred & twenty men, most of whom were white men & Negroes enlisted as sailors in the cities — And that such an expedition should be permitted to move forward in advance of the Army & in the midst of the enemy — It is sickening, deplorable, & makes me heart sick to think of these things — Pray with me — oh — I am so in with the Army — I think God if I will resign after this campaign, if not

You must avail yourself with your friends to obtain from the President to appoint J. D. W. for me. It is of the utmost importance to me — Give my love to Mrs Pierce & Lt & Mrs McNeil & I am if they are with you —

Your most affectionate
Brother — B. K. Pierce

To Hon. Franklin Pierce
U.S. Senate
Washington D.C.

FREE

Letter sent from St. Augustine, Florida, by B. K. Pierce to his brother, Franklin.

(From the original letter. Courtesy of the St. Lucie County Historical Museum.)

XIV   RETURN TO
MICHIGAN

Soon after the establishment of the supply depot at the Indian River Inlet, Colonel Pierce departed for St. Augustine. A Senator Pierce letter, dated January 27, states:

> *I have received a letter from Benjamin yesterday, dated the 12th instant at St. Augustine. He was there to procure supplies, transportation, etc., which had not been furnished as it should have been. He was in good health and was to return to his command at St. Lucie the next day.*

The "St. Lucie" reference suggests Pierce did not inform his brother about "Fort Pierce," probably assuming the post and honor bestowed upon him merely a temporary affair. St. Lucie County, in which the city of Fort Pierce is situated, perpetuates the designation by which the area was known at that time.

Pierce was delayed in his departure "by a long and severe storm which prevented me from getting out of this harbor on my return to my regiment," according to a letter he wrote January 24. In the same letter Pierce referred to news he received on a January 15 engagement by Lieutenant Powell with the Indians:

> *. . . on the St. Lucie River, and has been woefully whipped. My regiment, I presume, has marched before this to the scene of his battle, and I regret exceedingly that I am absent. . . . The 40 artillery with Powell belonged to our regiment, the 1st Artillery, and were nearly all killed and wounded and left upon the field.*

Pierce's information was inaccurate. According to army surgeon Motte, Lieutenant Powell's loss was five killed and twenty-two wounded. Colonel Pierce's artillery detachment conducted themselves honorably under the command of Lieutenant Fowler "whose gallant conduct covered the retreat of the sailors," and ". . . the whole command was saved from total annihilation."

In the January 24 letter, Pierce stated: "I think General Jesup will resign after this campaign, if so you (his brother, Senator Franklin) must exert yourself with your friends and obtain from the President the appointment of Quartermaster General for me.''

Pierce's prediction about General Jesup was correct. He resigned and was replaced by General Zachary Taylor, May 15, 1838. His brother was unable to obtain the Quartermaster General assignment for Benjamin, despite his obvious qualifications for that duty. It must be noted that similar to his previous assignments in the Seminole War, Colonel Pierce was again carrying a duel responsibility: supply and combat officer. He was equipped and ready to fight if the supplies in his care were threatened.

No letter or other information has been located so far indicating the precise date of Pierce's departure with the supplies for Fort Pierce, following the January 24th storm.

In preparation for a march inland, and while awaiting the supplies from St. Augustine, General Jesup and his troops, accompanied by Surgeon Motte, moved south a short distance to Jupiter Inlet and erected Fort Jupiter.

On January 26, General Jesup reported: "I shall be compelled to await (at Jupiter) supplies from Fort Pierce." Motte's Journal is more specific:

> *We were delayed here several days, before our preparations were completed for again taking the field. The principal cause of delay was the destitute condition of the troops. . . . On the 27th, when out of forage, and but two days' rations remaining on hand, Major Kirby and Lieutenant Powell fortunately arrived in barges with the First Artillery; bringing supplies from Fort Pierce. . . . On the 5th Febr'y, the shoes and every other necessary thing having arrived, we took up the line of march in pursuit of the enemy.*

From those notes it appears Colonel Pierce returned to Fort Pierce late in January or early February, and most probably accompanied the last of his supplies to Fort Jupiter, where General Jesup was headquartered. Whether Pierce took part in the march inland "in pursuit of the enemy" remains unknown. However, he appeared to be well informed on what transpired. General Jesup's expected battle did not materialize. Instead, following several "pow-wows," a temporary truce was agreed upon by both sides. On February 11, General Jesup dispatched his Aide-de-Camp, Lieutenant Thomas B. Linnard, to Washington with details of the truce, possibly accompanied by Colonel Pierce and some of his artillery men for part of the way to St. Augustine.

In a letter to his brother, Franklin, dated April 3, 1838, Savannah, Georgia, he wrote: "I have just arrived here on my way to New York under the order I received at St. Augustine. The (Jesup) campaign is over and it would be truly fortunate if the Indians would make up their minds to remove peaceably and quietly to the West." In a Senator Pierce letter, April 6, was written: ". . . more than three weeks ago since an order was sent (from Washington) to Benjamin to repair to Fort Hamilton." That assignment terminated Colonel

Pierce's part in Florida's Second Seminole War, and his January-February trip to Fort Pierce was the last the Worthy Commander ever made to the place named in his honor.

The Pierce family correspondence furnished most of the information on Colonel Pierce following his return from Florida. Upon his return, he visited his father and mother at Hillsborough, New Hampshire, his children with the McNeils at Boston, and made several trips to Washington. A June 19 communication stated: " Benjamin has not written since he left Philadelphia." This was probably an indication that he was on another recruiting duty.

During the summer of 1838, Colonel Pierce returned to Michigan; whether it was another military assignment, or personal matters, is not known. In a letter dated at Bloomfield, Michigan, November 8, 1839, a prominent citizen of the area, Ezra Baldwin, in reply to an October 11 letter from Colonel Pierce, stated: "You wished me to let you know why I did not inform you when you were here in '38."

Baldwin had purchased Pierce's Birmingham, Oakland County, property at a tax sale on October 1, unknown to Pierce and without Pierce's knowledge that an "extra State tax" had been assessed on all Michigan property to pay the costs of the "Toledo War," a dispute between Ohio and Michigan over boundary lines. Baldwin informed Pierce, "The sale of lands, when sold for taxes, has two years redemption."

There is an excellent possibility that Pierce's 1838 journey to Michigan was a wedding trip to show his bride his property and perhaps induce her to make it her home. The bride was the "Miss R." (Louisa A. Read) mentioned several times previously in the Pierce family correspondence. No information has been located as to the time or place of Benjamin K. Pierce's third marriage, at age forty-eight, seven years following the death of his second wife, Amanda Boykin. One might conjecture that the marriage may have taken place in Baltimore.

The source of information on Pierce's marriage to Louisa A. Read is a letter he wrote from Plattsburg, New York, November 13, 1838, to his oldest daughter, Harriet, age 21, residing with the McNeils, at Boston; "Your mother and myself, pleased by the reception of a letter from you which we had been long expecting. . . ." In reference to his other children, he wrote: "Their mother will write to them" and "Why not write oftener to me and Louisa. . . . She (Louisa) also received a very pretty letter from our daughter Elizabeth." He concluded: "Louisa joins me in love and affection, Your affectionate father, B. K. Pierce."

XV   THE FINAL YEARS

The final years of Benjamin K. Pierce's military career followed a pattern of assignments from one post to another. On December 10, 1838, his mother died (age 70), followed by the death of his father, April 1, 1839 (age 82). In February, Pierce attended a meeting of the distinguished Cincinnati Military Society (Order) in Boston.

From Washington, D.C., December 19, 1839, Franklin Pierce informed his sister, Elizabeth (Mrs. John McNeil), at Boston, "I received a letter last night from our dear brother B. K. in which he says: "My dear Louisa is no better and I am under the most painful and growing apprehension that she will soon be summoned from this to a better world." Louisa died January 6, 1840. Her age at death, the cause of death, and the place of burial are unknown. So far as can be determined, Colonel Pierce was still stationed at Plattsburg. There is a possibility that Louisa A. Read was the daughter of a Judge Read, prominent in northern Florida, the Carolinas and/or Virginia (a conjecture only). A "General Read, of Florida" served under Call in the Second Seminole War, another possibility concerning Louisa.

In the fall of 1839, Colonel Pierce was ordered back to Florida, but according to Senator Pierce, "The orders for the 1st. Reg't of Artillery to repair to Florida have been countermanded . . . due to the state of affairs on our northern frontiers." Whatever the situation was, the First Artillery and its commander were ordered to Fort Houlton, Maine, from which post Pierce wrote, July 14, 1840, "I do not know whether we shall remain here this winter or not."

On October 21, 1840, his daughter Harriet, age 23, married Lieutenant J. B. Ricketts, United States Army. Her father's estimation of his new son-in-law was, "A very clever young man of most correct and exemplary habits, of most respectable connections . . . I think he will make a good husband."

The First Artillery remained at Houlton through the winter of 1840-41. "It is awful cold here today (March 12, 1841)," the commander wrote, "about 20 degrees below zero and blowing hard . . . five feet of snow . . . this is the end of the world." Colonel Pierce advised his sister Elizabeth, "in case of war with Great Britain, which I believe we shall have at some day not far distant," to leave Boston and reside at the old home in Hillsborough, New Hampshire. "You will there be as safe from war's alarms as at any other place that I know of; whereas, in case of war, you could not remain in Michigan."

From a note included in a May 31, 1841, letter to General John McNeil, "Tuesday, June 1st., we are here at Concord (Mass.) and we leave tomorrow morn at two o'clock for Birmingham." The purpose of the trip and who accompanied him was not disclosed. That visit appears to be the last Pierce made to his Michigan property. By June 19, he was back at Washington.

In October, 1841, Colonel Pierce became a grandfather. "Houlton, October 11, . . . all well except Harriet. On Sunday she released of a little daughter. She is very ill, not expected to live during the day. This morning, thanks to God, she is better . . . the little child is quite pert." November 15, "Harriet is restored to health . . . the little baby is right smart and very pretty. She has named her Elizabeth after Mrs. McNeil." From Pierce's comments it is obvious he was proud of and happy with his first grandchild. On February 3, 1842, he wrote, "My dear Sister, I have been remiss in writing . . . I had nothing to say except the death of Harriet's little babe, and Elizabeth (his daughter) communicated to you that distressing intelligence."

From Houlton, Maine, April 28, 1842, Colonel Pierce wrote to General McNeil, "I have just received the news of the death of General Fenwick. This occurrence will make me a full Lieutenant Colonel." Advancement in rank apparently was based on seniority. Pierce had completed thirty years of military service. A July 26 correspondence stated: "The President (Tyler) has established nine military Departments in the United States. General Eustis has one and has left here for his headquarters at Portland, Maine. I am promoted to this Regiment (4th. Regiment of Infantry) and am in command of this Post." (Fort Houlton).

Colonel Pierce wrote the following to his sister on January 7, 1843, from Portland, Maine:

> *My dear Sister, You will think it strange perhaps to find my letter dated here, but late last month I was ordered unexpectedly to repair without delay to this post and take command of the 6th Military Dept. of which this is Head-Quarters. I arrived here . . . yesterday with Elizabeth (his daughter) who is not in the enjoyment of good health.   . . . Gen. Eustis has left here for Florida on a Court of Inquiry and will not probably be back for a month or two.*

As commander of the Sixth Military Department, temporary or otherwise, Colonel Benjamin K. Pierce, age 53, was holding the highest military office of his career.

Presumably Pierce returned to his Houlton command following his Portland tour of duty. The clue to his next assignment is a Deed of Conveyance in which "Lt. Col. Benjamin K. Pierce, United States Army, now resident of Fort Adams, Rhode Island" sold "the entire 160 acres" of his Birmingham, Michigan, property to John McNeil (his brother-in-law) " in consideration of the sum of $2,500. . . . Said B. K. Pierce have hereunto set my hand and seal at Newport, Rhode Island, this 3rd. day of May, 1844."

Pierce's last assignment appears to have been back to his former command, Fort Hamilton, Governors Island, New York, headquarters of the First Artillery Regiment: ". . . the Island . . . continuing its status as an artillery stronghold through 1852." (15)

The genealogical records of Benjamin K. Pierce state he died at New York City. With that clue this obituary notice was located in the *New York Evening Post,* dated Tuesday, April 2, 1850: "Died: In this city, on the 1st instant, at 3 a.m., Lieut. Col. B. K. Pierce, 1st. Regiment U.S. Artillery." From the New York Municipal and Archives Center, this additional information: "Residence: 199 Green Street, Disease: Paralysis. Cemetery: Removed from city."

Locating Colonel Pierce's place of burial posed a considerable problem until a descendent of the Pierce family stated: "I have always been told he was buried on Governors Island." Inquiries directed to army departments finally verified that Pierce was, at the time of death, buried on the Island; however, because of the erosion of the land, the cemetery was discontinued and all interments moved to the National Cemetery at Cyprus Hills, Jamaica and Hale Avenues, Brooklyn, New York. On "Gravesite No. Officers - West - Grave No. 20," is a white marble marker bearing the inscription:

BENJAMIN K. PIERCE

New Hampshire

Lieut. Colonel

1st. U. S. ART'Y

April 1, 1850

On the reverse side is inscribed:

HIS DAUGHTER

According to cemetery burial records, that daughter was "Eliz. H. Pierce," that is, Elizabeth Harriet, his daughter by his second wife, Amanda Boykin, and the daughter to whom Pierce referred on January 7, 1843, at Portland, Maine, as "not in the enjoyment of good health."

Thus, the exit of Fort Pierce's Worthy Commander at the age of fifty-nine years and six months, completing thirty-eight years of military service to his country.

XVI PEOPLE
IN PIERCE'S LIFE

With "Grave No. 20 - Officer's Section," Cypress Hills Cemetery, one might reasonably close the cover on the biography of Lieutenant Colonel Benjamin K. Pierce and go on to other interests, but that action would be unfair to Our Worthy Commander. In delving into the history of an individual such as Pierce, one learns many things about him other than his military activities.

Also, having, perhaps, created a reader interest in other individuals who had a role in Pierce's life, some brief closing comments on each should not be out of context: for example, there is the fate of Osceola, Pierce's worthy opponent. The intrepid Osceola died, age thirty-four, on January 30, 1838, a prisoner at Fort Moultrie, South Carolina, after having been treacherously seized by United States forces while attending a peace parley under a truce agreement. From the artist Catlin, who painted a portrait of Osceola a few days before he died, there is left the following description: "This gallant fellow . . . is grieving with a broken spirit and ready to die . . . I am fully convinced from all I have seen and learned from the lips of Osceola" . . . and others, "that he is a most extra-ordinary man, and one entitled to a better fate."

Insofar as the Second Seminole War is concerned, as of August 14, 1842, there is this account:

It is hereby announced that hostilities with the Indians within the (Florida) Territory have ceased. Measures are taken to pass the few remaining within certain limits - - those in the far south immediately, those west of the Suwanee (River) in a few days, who, meantime there is every reasonable assurance, will continue inoffensively if not molested in their haunts. The lands thus temporarily assigned as their planting and hunting grounds are within the following boundaries.

Following a detailed definition of these boundary lines, is written: "The foregoing arrangements are in accordance with the instructions of the President of the United States."

Thus, there is recorded the termination of the war between the United States and Florida's Indians. Today, the descendants of those few hundred "unconquerables" who

69

refused to be moved west beyond the Mississippi reside "inoffensively" and isolated to themselves in Florida's famed Everglades on the Big Cypress and Brighton Indian Reservations, a greatly reduced area from the original boundary lines of 1842.

The United States Army listed its casualties in that conflict as: 1,468, detailed; Medical Staff, 10; Lieutenant Colonels, 3; Majors, 4; Captains, 20; Lieutenants, 37; Sergeants, 84; Corporals, 57; Privates, 1,253. From Col. Pierce's First Regiment of Artillery were listed: 65 casualties; from Second Artillery, 104; Third Artillery, 158; Fourth Artillery, 38. The cost of the war was estimated at between thirty to forty million dollars. No definite accounting of the cost was made; hence, the estimate.

Next, Franklin Pierce, the source of so much information on Colonel Pierce through the many Pierce family letters, becomes of interest. Franklin resigned from the United States Senate in 1842 to accept the position of District Attorney in New Hampshire. He enlisted as a private (1846) at the outbreak of the Mexican War, was promoted to Brigadier General (1847) "although without military experience," and, following the peace treaty, February 2, 1848, returned to the practice of law. Although no records have been located on the subject, Franklin most probably assumed the responsibility of his brother Benjamin's interment on Governors Island; perhaps, also, the burial of Benjamin's daughter Elizabeth. As a "dark horse" in the 1852 Presidential campaign, Franklin was elected fourteenth President of the United States, two years after his brother Benjamin's death. In his last years, he resided at his Concord, New Hampshire, home, "an amiable, honest, generous, modest, educated gentleman, beloved by his personal friends, but almost forgotten by his countrymen."

The personal tragedies which occurred in the lifetime of Benjamin K. Pierce have been duly recounted. However, intermixed with those tragedies were many disappointments, thwarted ambitions and desires, and in the final analysis, financial problems which seem to have beset him in his later years. Not the least of these were the expenses in the care and education of his children, left motherless three times, and frequently without a father, and constantly being shifted from one military post to another. It is not difficult to imagine the thoughts of Benjamin K. Pierce as he contemplated the possibility of his death in the Seminole War and what would happen to his son and four daughters, motherless at that time. Colonel Pierce had problems which should be viewed with a sympathetic understanding.

Perhaps one of Pierce's greatest disappointments was the final disposition of his Birmingham, Michigan, property ("his farm"), on which he set such great store. In 1837, he wrote: "It is beautifully situated and is very valuable. . . . If I could remain here I could make thirty thousand dollars on it." Seven years later, May 3, 1844, he was obliged to sell the property for $2,500, apparently in a settlement of financial obligations to his brother-in-law, General John McNeil, who was also in financial difficulties.

The immediate cause of Pierce's monetary problems was that he, similar to others throughout the country, was caught in a nationwide financial debacle and economic depression. Pierce wrote, "It appears to me that everybody is bankrupt and money has vanished from the country."

How Pierce became indebted to such an extent to his brother-in-law is not clear, but it appears he not only borrowed from General McNeil, but was also financially obligated to his sister, Mrs. McNeil, for the care of his children. Sometimes she cared for all of them; sometimes she had two or three, while someone else cared for the others.

Pierce had other assets besides his mortgaged Michigan land.

I left property two years ago (1840) for sale at Plattsburg, which remains unsold to this day. I sold to John McCann, at New Castle, Delaware, a lot of land for $300 . . . but in this I am disappointed - - he is unable to pay. . . . If I was in any other part of the country but this (Houlton, Maine), I could raise some money. I have been struggling to pay where I owe and where money is due me do not receive a cent. This state of things keeps me constantly distressed and painfully straightened in any pecuniary affairs. . . . I owe Mrs. McNeil about $100 for children which I will send her as soon as possible. . . . I have $23 . . . in the Bank of Michigan. It is said the bank is broken but I will give you an order for it - - get it if you can. . . . I will send you in a few days (April 18, 1842), if the Pay Master has any money, $200 . . . I am as hard pressed as any poor Devil need be.

Such were the economic conditions of the country in the 1842 period. Pierce's final years were not pleasant ones.

Fate decreed for Benjamin K. Pierce a limited married family life interspersed with periods when his duties separated him from his motherless children. Numerous comments in his letters reveal the problems involved and his solicitude for their well being. In 1837, he wrote, "I left Elizabeth and Amanda with Mrs. Choates. . . . Harriet and little Charlotte will remain with my most excellent good sister, Mrs. McNeil. . . . I am now at ease and happy in the knowledge that my children are comfortable and well taken care of."

November 15, 1840, from Houlton, Maine, he wrote,

. . . the little sisters, Amanda and Charlotte, tell them they must write to their sister Elizabeth. . . . Poor child, it is pretty hard to go and stay so long (at Washington) among strangers . . . if nothing occurs to prevent me, I will bring her here for a time next (summer) so that the sisters can all meet together once more.

Elizabeth suffered a prolonged illness which required special care. She died young and, as stated previously, was buried at her father's grave-site. From Houlton, on May 18, 1841, he wrote, "I have concluded to bring the two little children here with me. The poor little children want to come home. I wish very much to see them."

In 1840, regarding his son, he wrote, "How is Benjamin getting along (in school)? . . . I hope he will turn his attention closely to study and be enabled in a few years to commence a respectable if not distinguished career in some profession. . . . how do Amanda and Charlotte behave?"

The following letter was written on November 15, 1841:

How does Benjamin get along at West Point? I feel very anxious that he may succeed at West Point (Military Academy), but if he does not, that he may go to some place from home where he may be kept steadily at his studies until he obtains a good and liberal education. With a good education he can gain a living and be a respectable member of society.

In 1838, Pierce wrote his daughter Harriet, who was with the McNeils at Boston, "Could you not attend the day school with cousin Fanny and attend the English branches and the French. . . . I have always been anxious to have you become a good English and French scholar. . . . Pray be discreet, correct and amiable in your manners and conduct."

The depth of Benjamin K. Pierce's religious beliefs are best judged by the following excerpts from his letters: ". . . under the blessing of Providence, I hope . . . to see you next season" (with his bride, Amanda Boykin). On the news of his father's illness: "I pray most fervently to our heavenly Father to restore you to health and strength." Commenting on a veto on an action by Congress, he stated: "Mr. Tyler, our President, has done a great and glorious act. God bless him."

In honoring Benjamin K. Pierce as the namesake of the city of Fort Pierce, one should bear in mind the many personal sacrifices he made in the service of his country, which, in the final analysis, brought him to Indian River Inlet and the palmetto blockhouse which was dubbed Fort Pierce. It is hoped that this last chapter affords a more intimate insight into the character of Benjamin K. Pierce as a husband and father whose cup of grief and loneliness was too many time filled to overflowing.

There is in the Pierce genealogical records this final tribute: "He was a brave and accomplished officer and gentleman . . . exceedingly amiable and kind, was graceful in his manners, and everywhere he was known was loved and respected."

To Harriet Peirce
                    My Dear Daughter,

        I was happy to hear of the improvement
of your health — & I was particularly
pleased to observe the improvement
in your hand writing — I hope you
will behave like a good girl &
merit the esteem & love of your
grand Father & grand Mother — Be
good in all things — Read the bible
regularly & never do any thing that your
understanding tells you is wrong —
                    Yr affectionate Father
                    B K Pierce

A letter from Benjamin K. Pierce to his daughter, Harriet.

Benjamin K. Pierce at the Indian River Inlet in 1838.
(Painting by D. H. Bucklen. The Indian River Community College Learning Center.)

XVII   BENJAMIN K. PIERCE
- A SUMMARY

1790

August 29   Benjamin Kendrick Pierce was born in Hillsborough, N.H.

1807

Fall   B. K. Pierce enrolled at Dartmouth College.

1810

Pierce studied law with David Starret in Hillsborough, N.H.

1812

March 12   Anticipating War of 1812, Pierce enlisted in the United States Army; he was commissioned a First Lieutenant and assigned to the Third Regiment of Artillery.

1813

October 1   Pierce was promoted to Captain and assigned command of an artillery company.

1814

May 6   Pierce participated in the Battle of Oswego.

1815

July 6   Pierce ordered to Mackinac Island, Michigan.

1816

April 2   Pierce married Josephine La Framboise, Mackinac Island, Michigan.
May 12   Benjamin Pierce was placed in charge of Ft. Holmes, on Mackinac Island.

<u>1817</u>

September 21   Captain Pierce assumed command of Fort Mackinac.
A daughter, Harriet, was born.

<u>1818</u>

December 30   Pierce purchased 160 acres of forest land in the center of today's city of Birmingham, Michigan.

<u>1820</u>

November 24   Pierce's wife, Josephine La Framboise, died in childbirth, presumably. Son, Langdon, born; died a few days later.

<u>1821</u>

Late Fall   Pierce assigned to Pensacola, Florida at Fort San Carlos De Barrancas.

<u>1823</u>

June 8   Pierce married Amanda Boykin, in Shasta, Alabama.
October 1   Captain Pierce was promoted to Brevet Major.

<u>1824</u>

Pierce was reassigned to Norfolk, Virginia.

<u>1827</u>

May 1   Major Pierce purchased a home and lot in St. Augustine, Florida.

<u>1829</u>

Pierce was made permanent commander of Fort Delaware.

<u>1831</u>

January   Pierce's second wife, Amanda Boykin, died.
February 8   Fort Delaware was destroyed by fire.

<u>1836</u>

August 20   Pierce was ordered to Florida to close Fort Defiance.
August 21   Major Pierce encountered Osceola at Fort Drane.
October 8   Pierce joined forces with Governor Call at Fort Drane.
October   Major Pierce was breveted Lieutenant Colonel.
November 21   Pierce engaged Indians at Wahoo Swamp.

<u>1837</u>

April   Pierce took command of Fort Hamilton, New York.
November   General Alexander Macomb ordered Pierce back to Florida.

1838

January 2	Palmetto log blockhouse erected at Indian River Inlet. It was named Fort Pierce.
April	Pierce was reassigned to Fort Hamilton, New York.
Summer	Pierce married Louisa A. Read in Baltimore, Maryland.
December 10	Pierce's mother died.

1839

April 1	Pierce's father died.
Fall	Pierce was stationed at Fort Houlton, Maine.

1841

October	A granddaughter, Elizabeth, was born.

1842

April	Pierce was advanced to full Lieutenant Colonel.
July 26	Pierce replaced General Eustis as commander of Fort Houlton, Maine.

1843

January	Lieutenant Colonel Pierce took command of the 6th Military Department at Portland, Maine.

1844

Pierce was stationed at Fort Adams, Rhode Island.

1850

April 1	Lieutenant Colonel Benjamin K. Pierce died - New York City.

REFERENCES

1. Jacob R. Motte, *Journey Into Wilderness*. Ed. James F. Sunderman (Gainesville: University of Florida Press, 1963) p. 173.

2. Ibid. p. 176.

3. *The Farmers Monthly Visitor.* (Concord, N.H.: William P. Foster) April 15, 1839.

4. Edwin O. Wood, *Historic Mackinac.* (New York: Macmillan Co., 1918) Vol. I, p. 472.

5. Elizabeth T. Baird, *Early Days on Mackinac Island.* (Wisconsin Historical Collection) Vol. 14, p. 17.

6. Ibid. Vol. 19, p. 109.

7. Baird "Memoirs" is the same as *Early Days on Mackinac Island.*

8. *The Floridian.* (Tallahassee) October 1–22, 1821.

9. *American State Papers; Military Affairs.* (Washington, 1832–1860) Vol. III, p. 507.

10. Ibid. Vol. IV, p. 81.

11. Ibid. Vol. IV, p. 733.

12. Ibid. Vol. VI, p. 561.

13. John K. Mahon, *History of the Second Seminole War*. (Gainesville: University of Florida Press, 1967) p. 177.

14. *American State Papers*. Vol. VII, p. 695.

15. Anastasio Carlos Mariano Azoy, *Three Centuries Under Three Flags: The History of Governors Island from 1637.* (Governors Island, N.Y.: First Army Headquarters, 1951).

BIBLIOGRAPHY

American State Papers: Military Affairs.
7 Vols. Washington, 1832–1860.
Pierce references:

      II, pp. 456, 518, 841
      III, p. 507
      IV, pp. 72, 81, 252, 416, 666, 733
      V, pp. 106, 115–19, 138, 144, 612
      VI, pp. 19–23, 561, 824
      VII, p. 695

Azoy, Anastaso C. M., *Three Centuries Under Three Flags:*
    The History of Governors Island.
    Governors Island: First Army Headquarters, 1951.

Baird, Elizabeth T., *Early Days on Mackinac Island.*
    Madison: Wisconsin Historical Collections.
    Vol. 14.

Bemrose, John, *Reminscences of the Second Seminole War,*
    ed. John K. Mahon, Gainesville: Univ. of
    Florida Press, 1966.

Brown, George M., *Florida War Record.*
    St. Augustine: Record Printing Co., 1902.

The Floridian. Tallahassee, October 1–22, 1821.

Foster, William P., *The Farmers Monthly Visitor.*
    Concord, April 15, 1839.

Heitman, Francis B., *Historical Register and Dictionary of the U.S. Army.*
    Washington: Government Printing Office, 1903.

Mahon, John K., *History of the Second Seminole War.*
    Gainesville: Univ. of Florida Press, 1967.

Motte, Jacob R., *Journey Into Wilderness,*
    ed. James F. Sunderman.
    Gainesville: Univ. of Florida Press, 1903.

Pierce, Benjamin K., Family Letters.
    Fort Pierce: Historical Data Center,
    Indian River Community College.
    (Photocopys of Pierce's letters.)

Sprague, John T., *The Florida War.*
    Gainesville: Univ. of Florida Press, 1964.

U. S. Army Orderly Records, McNeil Papers-Orderly Books.
    Concord: New Hampshire Historical Society,
    1815-1825.

Wood, Edwin O., *Historic Mackinac.*
    2 Vols. New York: Macmillan, 1918. Vol. 1.

DATE DUE